IN CONCERT

FAVOURITE GIGS OF
IRELAND'S MUSIC COMMUNITY

SUPPORTING SYRIAN REFUGEES

COMPILED BY NIALL MCGUIRK & MICHAEL MURPHY

ISBN 978-09955475-0-6

Compiled by Niall McGuirk and Michael Murphy
Design & layout by Lorna Tiefholz
Printed by RV Print, Bray, Co. Wicklow, Ireland

www.hopecollectiveireland.com

Hope Publications: 31 Hazel Road, Donnycarney, Dublin 9
E-mail: Niall@thumped.com

FOREWORD

This started off as a simple idea: let's try to help the Syrian refugees. We saw the horrific images being displayed for public consumption around the world and felt compelled to do something. We turned to our community and asked them to assist us in putting this collection together. This is the second collection of responses; the first one was published as *'Hope #2 – What was your favourite gig?'* Our friends in the punk rock and DIY world are in that publication. This time around we looked to our friends closer to home, in Ireland's music community. We asked the question and the replies kept coming in.

Our simple idea didn't stay simple for long because of the generosity, creativity, responsiveness and good hearts of the many contributors. Thank you all sincerely for helping us with this.

You can see the people who rolled up their sleeves and wrote for this book in the following pages. In addition, other people played a key role in making this volume possible. Lorna Tiefholz very generously offered to do the design and layout, and was not only very generous with her time, and also patient and understanding. We are delighted that the book looks outstanding thanks to her. Miriam McGurk, Josephine Scott, Polly O'Donnell, Susan Whittred, Deirdre Fitzgerald and Peter Weadack were all supportive and helpful and opened doors for us. In particular, Tom Pollard and Colm Walsh spread the word and reached out to their many friends in Ireland's music scene. Russ Bestley offered support, advice and encouragement.

All of the contributors deserve to be acknowledged in greater detail than space allows here. In a way, that's OK; their recollections of some of their favourite gigs speak loudly about their love of music. The fact that they took time to write such wonderful reminiscences on behalf of displaced people geographically distant from them says a lot about their good hearts.

We hope that you enjoy reading about some of the much loved gigs from members of Ireland's music community. It was a thrilling to receive and read these contributions from musicians, authors, supporters and crucial behind-the-scenes members of that community. And we hope the contributors enjoyed mining their memories and recalling the gems they wrote about. Many thanks to everyone who supported this project by writing, reading and contributing.

Niall McGuirk and Michael Murphy 2016

CONTENTS

1.

TED CARROLL
(PROMOTER, MANAGER OF THIN LIZZY, OWNER OF ROCK ON RECORD SHOP, PROPRIETOR OF CHISWICK RECORDS)

10 OF THE BEST

Bill Haley & The Comets
Theatre Royal, Dublin, February 1957

The Beatles
Adelphi Theatre, Dublin, 7 November 1963

Them
Stella Ballroom, Mount Merrion, Co Dublin, 1965

Bob Dylan & The Band
Adelphi Theatre, Dublin, 1966

The Byrds
Middle Earth London, May 1968

Aretha Franklin
Hammersmith Odeon, London, May 1968

Ike & Tina Turner
Royal Ballroom, Tottenham. 21 March 1969

Allman Brothers Band / Stooges / Skid Row
East Town Theatre, Detroit, November 1970

Sex Pistols
Jubilee Boat Trip, River Thames, London, June 1977

The Rolling Stones
100 Club. Oxford Street, London, 31 May 1982

2.

JOE WEADICK
(RED SEVEN/COLUMBIA SHOWBAND),
RED SEVEN/COLUMBIA SHOWBAND,
GRESHAM BALLROOM, LONDON, 1963

During my time playing trombone with the Red Seven/Columbia Showband in the sixties I experienced many memorable performances at venues throughout the twenty six Counties, Northern Ireland and indeed England. To decide on the most enjoyable gig I must first put that era in context.

Visualise the dawning of a beautiful new cultural age of music and dancing in Ireland, awakened by the refreshing sounds and rhythms of rock and roll, the twist, county rock and various pop songs/ballads. Mostly recorded by American and English singers/musicians including Elvis Presley, Gerry Lee Louis, Johnny Cash, Roy Orbison, Chuck Berry, Buddy Holly, Jim Reeves, Cliff Richard, The Beatles, The Rolling Stones, Dave Clark Five… the list could go on and on. And as they gained popularity and expertise the successful Irish showbands produced their own records. We made six records from 1965 to 1969.

The 'Ballroom of Romance' type music of the fifties where bands/orchestras sat and read music to strict tempo arrangements made way for this new and exciting dance culture. The chairs were thrown away; 'sitting' gave way to 'standing'; and the band members moved to the rhythm of the music for the duration of the programme. The era of the 'Irish Showband' was born.

To say what my most enjoyable gig was is very difficult as I loved almost every performance even when things did not go as well as they might have. We believed in the saying 'the show must go on' and in creating a happy-go-lucky atmosphere on stage. We reckoned that positive vibes from the band rubbed off on the dancers and they responded in kind.

I would have to say on reflection that the most enjoyable gig I was involved in with the band was in 1963 in the Gresham Ballroom on Holloway Road London. We had played in most of the Irish ballrooms in that majestic city before then but this was the largest. There were somewhere between three and four thousand people at it and quite a number of them Irish fans of ours who were working in London. It had a unique revolving stage and the resident band played off while the stage turned around to expose us to the large crowd as we played *Deep in the Heart of Texas'* (a hit by Duane Eddy in 1962). We received a tremendous applause. It was an incredible experience for us at the time and for me personally really special. I was just coming up to my 21st birthday.

I would have to say that a close second to the remarkable night in London was in 1961 during our summer residency in the Tara Ballroom Courtown Co. Wexford – the most popular dance venue on the east coast outside Dublin at that time. It was a Sunday night at the height of the season and it was packed with about 1700 people. You could almost step on and walk along the shoulders of the dancers from the stage to the main door – similar to what Paul Hogan did in the film *Crocodile Dundee*!

Pete Coburn was our lead singer then and he sang, for the first time at a gig, Roy Orbison's new hit *'Only the Lonely'*. I got goose pimples just listening to him while helping the boys with the backing vocals. Pete got a tumultuous applause and it was requested many times – his voice was exceptional. During the song most of the dancers stopped and watched his beautiful rendition.

To add to that brilliant performance, on the same night, in true showband style, Pete and Pat Tyrrell sang and acted out the song *'Dr I'm in Trouble'* from the film *'Millionairess'* starring Sophia Loren and Peter Sellers. Pete put on a dress and sang Sophia Loren's part while Pat sang Peter Seller's part. At the end of the performance Pete ran across the stage and jumped into Pats waiting arms. Magnificently done and again a very large crowd stood around the stage thoroughly enjoying the sketch. This was one of many such sketches we performed over the years.

3.

MARCUS CONNAUGHTON
(BROADCASTER, AUTHOR, RORY GALLAGHER – HIS LIFE AND TIMES, SAILING BY – A CELEBRATION OF 25 YEARS OF SEASCAPES)
FLEETWOOD MAC
DUBLIN, 1969

For a teenager hungry to hear great musicians and emerging artists generally heard of by word of mouth – the National Boxing Stadium on Dublin's South Circular Road was the place to be in the sixties, seventies and eighties. It was in this venue that I was "steeped" (in Cork "haunted") to see Rory Gallagher with Taste (the second line-up with John Wilson and Richard McCracken); Planxty; John Mayall and his Bluesbreakers; Led Zeppelin; Leonard Cohen; Eric Clapton; Ry Cooder; Thin Lizzy; Skid Row; Vinegar Joe; Jethro Tull; Kid Creloe and the Coconuts and the dazzling Peter Green and Fleetwood Mac to name just a handful. Fleetwood Mac's repertoire was drawn from the work of the great Chicago urban bluesmen and was dominated by the exquisite playing of Danny Kirwan and Jeremy Spencer crowned by the effortless artistry of Peter Green on his Gibson Les Paul.

On the night they played the National Boxing Stadium in the round they were supported by one man band, the late Duster Bennett and the performance stands out as one of the stellar shows by the real Fleetwood Mac, when 'Albatross', 'Need Your Love So Bad' and 'Green Manalishi' were staples on their set list. With a rhythm section of John McVie on bass and Mick Fleetwood on drums who had served their apprenticeship in the Bluesbreakers with John Mayall, they sparkled. Indeed it's a very close run thing that the night that Yes, The Bonzo Dog Doo Dah Band and The Nice played to a packed Stadium they get pipped at the post by Greeny's Fleetwood Mac.

4.

BRIAN O'KEALLAIGH
(THE GOREHOUNDS, RECORD SHOP PROPRIETOR, IRISH RECORD FAIRS)
GOOSE LAKE INTERNATIONAL MUSIC FESTIVAL
MICHIGAN, 1970

What was your favourite gig? What a question! How does one define favourite when there have been so many good, even great, gigs, with so many classic performances and unique settings?

Should I choose the Specials at the Olympia, where we left drenched to the bone from the packed sweaty jumping joy-fest that was their return Dublin gig, or at the same venue, Kraftwerk, leaving me deaf for two days afterwards when I worked my way to the front to revel in their *Mensch Machina*? Could it be…Ramones (DEF my fave signing session!) at the TV Club, Zappa & Bonzos in Ravinia, Gladiators in Trinity, Carnsore, Electric Picnic, gosh so many, going back so so far, lol ??

I guess I should tip my hat to my generation and go back, way back in time

I suppose the denominator that decides the all time favourite gig is the one that brings the most memories that last, and for me that must be my very first festival, when I hitched 300 miles at age 16 to Goose Lake, Michigan in the hot sunny summer of 1970, August 7-9. The line-up was a Who's Who of Rock at the time: including the Faces with Rod Stewart and Ronnie Wood, the James Gang, Chicago, 10 Years After, John Sebastian, Bob Seger, Mountain, Paul Butterfield Blues Band, the Stooges, Flying Burrito Brothers, Savage Grace, Mitch Ryder, the MC5 and the icing on the cake was undoubtedly the final act on the final night, Jethro Tull, just breaking in a new pianist, John Evan, who played a mesmerising 20, or was it 30, minute solo on two grand pianos at the same time. They stayed for 4 or 5 encores and 2 and a half hours.

More than 200,000 people were at the Goose Lake International Music Festival, but you would never have guessed, the vibe was completely peaceful, there was none of the ubiquitous American Police presence, and everybody was free to do whatever they wanted, as long as you kept the Peace, Man.

Booths lined the walkways either side of the revolving stage where drugs of all types were available, the lake provided ample opportunities for skinny dipping, the sun was eternal, the music rocked and Hells Angels mixed with hippies without any hint of hassle. In a section where giant tri-wheeled chopper hogs were gathered the Angels looked on with head scratching scorn as about 30 white suited musicians filed onto a stage to line up behind waist high white stands.

Then a curtain was drawn and a giant double bass drumkit was revealed. Buddy Rich came out, and slayed us all with his one handed rolls and solos that were so varied that five or ten minutes passed as if they were one or two. I looked around and the Hells Angels' jaws were dragging on the ground in amazement – they had never heard this Big Band stuff before, and they were enjoying it!

Iggy roared and groaned and made us all feel the pain, and the joy. Headbanging to 10 Years After and Mountain. Even Rod rocked at the peak of the Faces career. Joe Walsh really was something, a brilliant guitarist and, like so many 3 piece groups have done (Nirvana at the Top Hat, another contender for fave), made the hairs on my neck stand up with his powerful guitar and backing group, the James Gang. It was all about the music and it wasn't just about the music.

Chatting, swimming, walking around just feeling the love, political nous and peace movement vibe and utter freedom that was at that festival, doing the things 16 year olds do, was a total experience for three days. And it was even better than Woodstock the year before, there was no rain!

5.

FERDIA MACANNA
(ROCKY DE VALERA, THE RHYTHM KINGS, AUTHOR, THE ROCKY YEARS)
THIN LIZZY
DUBLIN, 1971

In February 1971, Thin Lizzy played a week of lunchtime gigs at the Peacock theatre, Dublin. My school pals and I sneaked out of Colaiste Mhuire early each day (it was called 'going on the bounce') to see our favourite band. Lizzy were the only local superstars you could bump into on the street who were happy to chat and sign autographs for smart-alec acne-headed rock struck fifteen years old Dublin kids.

The first gig was Thursday 25th and admission was our lunch money - 25 pennies. The audience consisted mostly of longhairs, almost but obscured by clouds of thick and tangy weed smoke.

Phil Lynott, Brian Downey and Eric Bell started rocking at 12.45. The highlight was their blistering fifteen minute version of the stage fave, *'Ray Gun'*. Then to the surprise of the longhairs in the audience, the band gave way to the Abbey Theatre players who performed an extract from *'The Plebians Rehearse the Uprising'* by Gunther Grass. Once the play started, the hippies barrelled off and only returned when Lizzy came back on to play their second and last set.

On the Friday, the instant Lizzy finished their first set, Phil Lizzy grabbed the mic and ordered the audience to remain seated and watch ' the fookin' play cos' it's fookin' art'. Nobody budged. The play extract received respectful and even warm applause. The Friday gig was my favourite. I remember the sensation of returning late to school (sneaking in through he bicycle shed) and being so high on rock and roll and deafened by Bell's lead guitar and Lynotts thunderous bass and Downey explosive drumming that I couldn;t hear a word of the double science class. It was the most exciting afternoon 0f my teenage life.

Years later, I met Lynott. When he discovered that my father was Tomas Mac Anna, the Abbey theatre producer who had promoted the Peacock gigs, he shook my hand and announced ' your dad is a fookin' legend'.

I still listen to *'Ray Gun'* off their first LP, though I remember the shock when I bought the album only to discover that the tune was now only around two and a half minutes long. They had given us the true version in those Peacock gigs and I was lucky to have been there.

6.

GERRY MCAVOY
(RORY GALLAGHER BAND, AUTHOR)
RORY GALLAGHER
BELFAST, 1971

I'm sitting in a dressing room in Bavaria Germany, waiting for the soundcheck to happen. Anyway here we go my most memorable show with Rory.

It was 1971,the same year I joined Rory. We had been touring around Europe and USA since April of the same year. We finished the year with 3 shows in Ireland - Belfast, Dublin and Cork. Belfast was the show I was looking forward to, both with excitement and in trepidation. The excitement, because Belfast is my hometown and I was returning as the bass player with one of top guitarists in the world. In trepidation because in 1971 Belfast was under high alert because of The Troubles (the most common name for the day to day violence and bombings that had become commonplace in the 6 counties).

Also we were told the show was a sellout. Firstly because it was the first time Rory had returned to Belfast, after the demise of his previous band Taste. Secondly because named bands from the UK and further afield would not travel to Northern Ireland because of The Troubles. Before the show we were sitting in the dressing room and we could feel the anticipation from the audience. About 15mins before stage time the audience began their chant "Rory, Rory, Rory". Then it was time to go.

When we hit the stage, the roar from the audience was incredible. This lasted for more than 2 minutes. Rory kicked off and we sailed through a 3 hour set meaning that transport for most of the audience would have stopped by 10pm, yet again because of the situation in Belfast. Not one person left the venue (Ulster Hall) until the concert finished, which was well after 11pm. Even then a lot of the fans queued up outside the dressing room for autographs and hello's.

When it all died down and we got back to our hotel The Europa (by the way the most bombed hotel in the world at that time). Our promoter (the late great Jim Aiken) informed us that unbeknown to us 3 bombs had gone off in the city centre during our concert, and only a few streets away from the Ulster hall. Unbelievable. What a night

7.

JOHN MCKENNA
(BROADCASTER)
LEONARD COHEN
DUBLIN, 1972

It was an evening in March 1972 at the National Stadium in Dublin. I was a student at the time but, as a relatively recent convert, I'd managed to scrape together the money for a ticket to the first of his two shows that evening. As I was hedging my bets and trying not to leave the Stadium after the first show, I met a fellow student, Luigi Rea, whose family was involved in the catering for the gigs. I told him my predicament and, kind man that he was, he managed to get me out and then back into the venue- as an instant member of the catering staff - for the second show.

That was the night Cohen sang *Kevin Barry* to the amazement and delight of the gathered throng. I've had the pleasure seeing and interviewing him many times since but there's nothing that beats that night for atmosphere and excitement. Then, I remind myself, those were the days when bands were slow to come to Ireland and seeing someone like Leonard Cohen had the possibility of being a once (or in that case, twice) in a lifetime experience.

8.

PETE HOLIDAI
(THE RADIATORS, TROUBLE PILGRIMS)
ALICE COOPER [ORIGINAL BAND]
THE KILLER TOUR SUPPORTED BY ROXY MUSIC
LONDON, 1972

The week leading up to the gig took a life changing twist when Roxy Music, who had just released their debut album and appeared on their now legendary performance on The Old Grey Whistle Test, was announced as the opening act.

Arriving early to catch their set Roxy Music made a lasting impression on me with their blend of futuristic space age art rock. It was obvious even then that Brian Eno's understated stage presence was always going to catch the eye. Sonically Roxy were like and electronic jukebox pumping out catchy riffs and experimental noisescapes in equal measure.

The Alice Cooper band had developed from similar art rock roots and morphed into a theatrical experience that was on the cusp of megastardom. The band retained their hard rock attitude driven by those Gibson SG guitars and augmented by 'Alice's persona of shock rocker. This particular tour saw Alice 'chopping' a baby with an axe, with copious amounts of fake blood that would guarantee your girlfriend hid and hugged you for protection. As in most good theatre a suitable punishment to fit the crime had to be devised and low and behold a gallows seemed to appear from nowhere and Alice was hung by the neck, including a neck break audio through the PA. In a flash the band were back with *We've Still Got A Long Way To Go*, where Alice wore a white top hat and tails as if in a Busby Berkley Hollywood film.

I remember it all as if it was yesterday.

Set List: *Be My Lover*
You Drive Me Nervous
Yeah, Yeah, Yeah
I'm Eighteen
Halo of Flies
Dead Babies
Long Way to Go
School's Out
Is It My Body
Under My Wheels

9.

CIARAN O'NEILL
(THE UNDERTONES, THAT PETROL EMOTION, EVERLASTING YEAH)
PLANXTY
DERRY, 1973

Christy was sweating bullets; I know because he was standing at a microphone an arm's length away from me. Eyes shut, red faced, skin as slick as an ice cube coated in mercury. He was singing from another place, peppering the smoky air with flecks of spittle. It was 1973, St. Columb's Hall in Derry and Planxty were in town. The classic line-up of Moore, Lunny, O'Flynn and Irvine - the Brazil '70 of Irish traditional music. No parking the tour bus and playing for a draw here - it was the beautiful game from the off.

I was 10 years old, a backstage freeloader courtesy of my uncle Liam who was operating the 3 colour lighting rig. Raised with The Beatles and The Stones and a recent convert to the Church of Ziggy this was not rock 'n roll as I knew it. But in a different way it absolutely WAS - a rebel yell in a town made callous, still emotionally shut down just over a year after Bloody Sunday.

Memory is a slave to time and recollections of the evening are now hazy but like a first kiss the detail is secondary, the consequences imperishable. What matters is the feelings engendered - the elevation, the sense of possibility and freedom - all the things that music should bring. When Planxty played *Tabhair Dom Do Lamh* the beauty was bombproof - O'Carolan's sad sweet refrain on the uileann pipes breaking your heart and healing it at the same time like wordless Celtic gospel music. I saw them again a year later in Buncrana with Johnny Moynihan replacing Donal Lunny and they were probably even better but the Derry gig is the one that tugs at me. As Louis MacNeice might have put it 'the first blossom was the best blossom'.

10.

NEIL MCCORMICK
(AUTHOR, JOURNALIST, HOT PRESS, DAILY TELEGRAPH, MEMBER OF SHOOK UP!, AUTHOR OF KILLING BONO)
U2
DUBLIN, 1976

You always remember your first time. The first rock show for me was 1976 in the school gymnasium at Mount Temple in Dublin, when four of my fellow students in a band called Feedback got up on some taped together tables and played a short set of Peter Frampton, Beach Boys and Bay City Rollers songs that sent a lightning bolt through my teenage psyche. I had seen some folk music over the years but never an electric amplified band and I honestly have never recovered. The band changed their name to U2 and I've been watching them ever since, along with the rest of the world.

Whatever performer's instinct is in Bono, that big hungry heart that can never be filled was already present in 1976. When he grabbed a mic stand, stomped on the tables and roared "I want you, show me the way!" it just shook the room and sucked everyone into his world. Schoolgirls were screaming. Schoolboys were punching the air in delight. By any objective criteria, they must have been pretty shaky, but none of us knew any better. It was a life-changing gig, for them and for me. Over the next few years in Dublin, I watched them turn into a white hot rock band in pubs, clubs, community centres and church halls, and those shows are seared in my mind forever, the thunder of Adam and Larry's rhythm section, the sci-fi wonder of Edge's echoing guitar orchestra, and the inchoate humanity of Bono stumbling towards stardom. But I saw them again this week, in the O2 Arena London, and was picked up and blown away all over again. It is rock theatre of the highest order, a heart bursting drama of emotional politics. Bono opened his soul and communed with 20,000 people, turning a multitude into one.

I remember thinking that this was the best I had ever seen them, and then laughing at myself, because I think that every time I see them. U2 make live music that is actually live to the moment, music that renews with every performance. Live doesn't get better than that.

11.

DAVE SWEENEY
(THE MAX QUAD BAND, ROCKY DE VALERA AND THE GRAVEDIGGERS, THE FAT LADY SINGS)
DR FEELGOOD
DUBLIN, 1976

National Stadium, October 20 1976

Myself and my good friend Tony were mad music fans and big NME readers. Something new and dangerous was brewing out there in musicland and Dr Feelgood were at the centre of it. We had to see them live somehow. The problem was that there were no big rock gigs in Dublin other than local heroes Horslips and the annual Rory Gallagher fest at the Carlton Cinema in O'Connell Street. Random glimpses of Dr. Feelgood and the New York Dolls on BBC television was the best we could hope for.

Tony and I were discovering alcohol. It was difficult to get. The Pirates Den bar was in a cellar, dark and mysterious and if we got the right barman, he would serve us rum and blacks. One Saturday night we crept in as usual and did a double take. There was a poster on the front door. "UCD Students Union presents Doctor Feelgood at the National Stadium" !!! We couldn't believe it – we thought it was the rum – we'd already had some at O'Briens pub. We went back outside and looked again. It was unbelievable but true. The Feelgoods were coming! We bought our tickets the next day.

"The Stadium", - the national boxing stadium - was a seedy place with cinema seats except where there were some folding chairs – the best seats and right by the stage – these chairs took the place of the boxing ring when gigs took place. It was a perfect venue, slightly run down, with great sound and the stage never too far from the punters. It did also have a small army of white coated no nonsense bouncers whose normal role was keeping order at vicious and bloody fistfights. Rock and roll fans seemed fair game to these guys.

The place was packed. We sat and waited topping up our stadium orange juice from small bottles hidden in our socks. The support act was the Arthur Phybes Band with a singer in a bowler hat. Not bad. They finished. We waited. We were more than ready. Hold on? Were the Feelgoods really in Dublin? Were they really here?

The house lights went down. The place went crazy. Dark shadows and someone in a white jacket moved across the stage. "I said, heeyyyy, everybody (clang) all around the room..!" They were here in Dublin, straight from Canvey Island – the Feelgoods, opening up with the title track of their just released, soon to be number one, live album, *'Stupidity'*. Their incendiary frontman Lee Brilleaux, stage centre, in a dirty white dinner jacket, staring out with a manic gaze, growling his vocals, singing as if his life depended on it. The explosive guitarist Wilco Johnson with his dark shirt and dark Telecaster storming around the stage playing Chuck Berry on sulphate riffs - with no plectrum – and straight into a H and H IC 100 amplifier. No flash effects pedals just a curly guitar lead and an incomparable style. Behind the frontmen was the most rock solid rhythm section bringing it all home all the time and totally 'in the pocket'. Dark suited and looking hungover. On the right the moustacheiod John B Sparks on bass and flared trousers and behind was the indescribable rhythmic presence of the truly legendary and slightly terrifying Feelgoods drummer, the Big Figure.

This was incendiary rock and roll, the like of which I have never seen since. The great songs kept coming, the excitement and passion kept building. *'Back in the Night'* with Brilleaux on slide guitar. *'She Does It Right'*, *'I'm a Hog For You Baby'*, *'Going Back Home'*, *'I Can Tell'* The heavy stadium bouncers were getting very worried indeed and struggled in vain to keep order. This was becoming riotous. The folding chairs were flying.

Everytime Wilco took a solo he would run out from side to side across the stage, the crowd went berserk and stood up as a man (there were no women). It was if every time Wilco went on one of his runs we all celebrated that yes!, the Feeelgoods, were actually here, in long suffering Dublin. Now that I think of it it the nearest thing I experienced to those Wilco runs were and are the memorable Irish football goals against England, Italy and Germany. Even those great moments could not match Wilco that night.

The more manic Wilco got, the more Lee Brilleaux stood rooted to the spot, hogging the microphone and staring out into space. He ignored Wilco. There was never any eye contact beween them and they never exchanged a word.

The gig continued. An hour or so went by. Suddenly it was time for *'Riot In Cell Block Number 9'* machine gun guitar from Wilco and a staccato reverb laden narrative vocal from Brilleaux echoed around the hall bringing us straight to Rikers Island. Then it was over. We roared and shouted. We knew we would never see the like again. Would they come back for another song? Yes they would. *'Route 66'* was one of the encores, then they were gone leaving devastation all around.

Before punk, the Ramones, the Pistols, the Clash there was the immortal Feelgoods. They made waves everywhere and for my money punk rock would not have happened without them. Locally Bob Geldof's new band the Boomtown Rats played the entire Feelgoods first album in their live set.

For me that Stadium show was the real beginning, I had to play rock and roll guitar with a strong dose of Wilco. I did and it took me everywhere after that October night long ago. Definitely the best rock gig I have ever seen.

12.

TONY CLAYTON-LEA
(DJ, AUTHOR, JOURNALIST, THE IRISH TIMES)
IGGY POP
LONDON, 1977

39 years? No, don't be ridiculous! It couldn't be. It simply couldn't. Er, actually, hold on a cotton-pickin' minute, I do believe it is 39 years to the season that I first saw not only my first life-changing gig, but the event that kickstarted a cultural revolution in my head. It was Iggy Pop, in London, at a venue that was then called the Rainbow Theatre but which is now a building belonging to the Brazilian Pentacostalist Universal Church of the Kingdom of God. Not to worry – a religious experience is a religious experience whatever the venue.

Back then, I had short hair, wore straight-legged jeans and Doc Marten boots. *NME* was my weekly bible of cultural reference points – anything that Charles Shaar Murray, Nick Kent, Tony Parsons or Julie Burchill recommended to read/see/hear I'd do just that. London is a mind-expanding city at any time, of course, but in 1977/78? Well, wasn't that was a time and a place for a young lad to live in, his head spinning from the amount of music to experience and the sights to see.

Punk rock hadn't yet levelled out to become a caricature of itself; there were no ostrich-coiffured punks strolling along King's Road or Camden High Street tapping tourists for money. The music was the thing, and from my experience, at least, it was as close to the real deal anyone from a provincial Irish town could imagine. Seeing Iggy Pop headline in a major London venue at around the time when punk rock was at its most influential seemed just that little bit more exciting. And besides, what wasn't to love about milling into the tube station at Finsbury Park with several hundred Stooges fans singing '*Your Pretty Face is Going to Hell*'?

Fact is, I recall that gig as if it were last night: from the early 70's, Iggy Pop had been given a new lease of life via his friendship with David Bowie, and Pop's proto-punk band The Stooges had attained an enviable high regard from London's leading punk rock acts. But it was as much Iggy as the music that the audience was into: I've never seen anyone before or since utilise their body as if it were pliable work of art. Bowie's lyric from the '*Ziggy Stardust*' album track, '*Hang On To Yourself*', about moving "like tigers on Vaseline" could have been written about Pop, for he slithered around, prowled, on that stage, barracking and beckoning the crowd to do things that, collectively, an audience really shouldn't. There is something incredibly compelling about a performer that seems to care little about their physical well being; it's a car-crash scenario that sucks you in, and when the performer is as fearless as Pop an element of genuine danger gets dragged kicking and screaming into a heady mix that includes potent rock music, stimulants of varying kinds and the sense that all of the audience are misfits or miscreants just like you.

I remember leaving the venue and walking towards the tube station, jostling my way past other fans, and thinking not only how invincible was my belief in the power of brilliant music, but also how invulnerable that belief made me feel. 35 years later I still feel the same (performing pop clowns notwithstanding), but I have often asked myself why is that the case? What is it about the live music experience that continues to scratch at what is clearly a severe itch?

13.

DAMIAN O'NEILL
(THE UNDERTONES, THAT PETROL EMOTION, EVERLASTING YEAH)
SIOUXSIE & THE BANSHEES, THE HEARTBREAKERS
MANCHESTER, 1977

It's September 4 1977 and myself, my brother Vinny and our friend Eugene have endured an arduous overnight boat trip from Larne to Liverpool and then bus to Manchester with one aim in mind- to finally pop our punk cherry on foreign soil and see Johnny Thunders and the Heartbreakers supported by Siouxsie and the Banshees at Manchester's Umist.

We get to the venue early in anticipation that it could sell out but we needn't have worried. The doors were already open and so we sauntered in (free of charge) straight to the front of Johnny's side of the stage.

A good omen of what was to follow.

By the time the Banshees hit the stage the place was jammed.

Siouxsie Sioux came out wearing her famous tits t-shirt and with not so much as a hello the Banshees blasted through an intense and blistering set that we later found out included songs like *'Metal Postcard'*, *'Love In A Void'*, *'Overground'* and *'Hong Kong Garden'*.

This was the original line up so we were lucky to witness them before Kenny Morris and Steve McKay abruptly left the band just two years later.

Siouxsie strutted the stage yelping and goose stepping, a memorising performer.

They disappeared as quickly as they came on leaving us exhausted and feeling we'd been run over by a bullet train.

A short time later the Heartbreakers swagger onstage and there he is, just two feet in front of me and I'm pinching myself.... Johnny Thunders, guitar hero, New York Doll!

"This numbers called Born to Looossseeee...." he drawls in his finest Queens, Noo York accent and proceeds to let rip into the mean and dirty opening guitar riff on his battered Gibson Les Paul Jr. and suddenly I know I am witnessing something special and will never be quite the same again.

The Heartbreakers were on fire that night, no junkie business here thank you very much. My 16 year old self is captivated and enthralled by the aural and visual wonderment that is before me.

Johnny and Walter Lure stagger round the stage swapping guitar solos and vocal duties whilst bassist Billy Rath keeps it nailed down tight and of course Jerry Nolen, another ex-New York Doll himself, with his bleached blond hair, keeping it all together seamlessly behind his huge drum kit.

Little did we know that the band were falling apart and that Jerry would quit a few weeks later. Maybe they got rid of all their frustrations that particular night in Manchester in the way they knew best. Who knows?

They quickly rip through virtually every great song from the recently released *'LAMF'*... *'Pirate Love'*, *'All By Myself'*, *'Get Off The Phone'*, *'One Track Mind'*, *'I Wanna Be Loved'*, *'Chinese Rocks'* and we're pogoing to every song, the sweat pouring out of us, laughing and having the time of our lives.

They encore with *'Chatterbox'* and suddenly the lights go on and we stagger out soaking wet into the murky September night. My life has been changed forever.

14.

JUDE CARR
(HEAT FANZINE)
THE RADIATORS FROM SPACE
DUBLIN, 1977

A message outta the blue from Michael…Write a few words about Your Favourite Gig…. It sounded like homework… the hound dog ate my ecker. Christian Brudders.

I agreed as it's such a great cause but Whitney we have a problem…. I can't put my arms around a memory… I went, saw, dug and partied… but I took no notes.

Mid/late 70's Dublin was a fairly desolate place… Rory, Lizzy and Horslips. I never got Gallagher. It was black and white…. Our world had not yet gone dayglo. Punk arrived…. We were saved!!!

Eddie and the Hot Rods and Dr Feelgood were the early outriders….They had energy and didn't rely on wasp in a jam jar guitar solos.

The Clash played back to back gigs in Trinity….the first one was the better. That was some gig.

The Ramones played Phibsboro…. Rewind… The Ramones played Phibsboro! The State Cinema where as a kid I had seen Darby O Gill and the Little People (a movie not a Boston garage punk band).

Belfield Burnin was a Punk gig where it went wrong… A boy Patrick Coultry got murdered, Punk got blamed..It was a difficult time. Me and Pete, were disc spinners that night.

Fast forward to the most important gig of all time…..Jimmy …drum roll please…..

Morans Hotel…. A new house record. *Heat* our fanzine, called it "Punks first night out since Belfield". It was the debut of the new four piece Radiators from Space, and the Rads farewell to the Emerald Isle. It included The Fabulous Fabrics…who were playing their first gig days after buying guitars in Woolworth (whatever happened to them? Woolworth I mean). The Vipers and Revolver completed the support. Billy from Revolver was one of the coolest cats I have ever met.

The Radiators invited Steve back on stage at the end. They belted out *'I Feel Alright'* by Iggy and the Stooges. Our world was back as it should be, we could all move on.

Later Dublin hosted gigs by The Only Ones, XTC, Elvis and the Buzzcocks.

Heat got into a spot of bother with a local band…. They had yet to release a record. The High Court agreed we damaged their career. In a roundabout way it led to another classic gig…. For one night only The Defenders at the National Ballroom. Paul, Donal and Bill R.I.P. and thanks.

Shortly afterwards I ran away from the circus.

15.

AIDAN O'ROURKE
(THE SINNERS)
THE CLASH
DUBLIN, 1977

The gig I remember most from my time in Dublin in the late 70s was the concert by The Clash in the magnificent and ornate Examinations Hall of Trinity College Dublin. Previously it had only been used for exams and other ceremonial functions but - if I remember correctly - ENTS - TCD's student-led entertainments organisation - had pushed for it to be used for music concerts. I wondered if the stucco would fall off the ceiling with the noise or if the condensation would damage the walls.

On the day I saw the articulated lorries parking outside as they set up the stage and the amplification equipment. That evening, The Clash exploded into action. This was a far cry from a basement club. The cacophony echoed around the huge hall, it was just a mass of noise. Joe Strummer struck poses, hollering into the microphone like someone filled with anger. There were lots of people there but the hall was by no means full. Despite the bad acoustics, it was a great gig and very memorable - I remember it now! I spent some time up at the front then wandered down to the back end of the hall.

Finally the concert was over and we all filed out through the door and out onto Front Square. After that it might have been the Buttery or if it was too late, somewhere else - the Bailey perhaps - I can't remember! Later I did my finals in this hall, and in 2002 I received my MA degree certificate from Mary Robinson there, but I will never forget the deafening, echoing, explosive entity that was the Clash playing in TCD Exam Hall in 1977.

16.

JAKE REILLY
(THE BLADES)
THE CLASH
DUBLIN, 1977

In the summer of 1977, Years before I met Paul Cleary and joined The Blades I was working in Leighton Buzzard. I used to get the train down to London for the weekends, stay in a mate's flat in Chelsea and hang around the King's Road. I remember the piles of rubbish in the sweltering heat and of course the punks; I loved the laugh out loud, in your face…ness of The Sex Pistols. I remember being in a record store in Leighton Buzzard and being told; "Buy the bleedin' single or get out" after asking the assistant to play *'Complete Control'* for the tenth time!' Topper Headon's drumming left me in awe.

Back in dirty Dublin suddenly everyone was forming bands, gigs were being staged in The Project Arts Center and The Dandelion Market. Macdonald's opened on Grafton Street and instantly became a hang-out for shorthaired, wiry kids with skinny jeans and bright socks and brothel creepers or docs.

But ground Zero was that night in Trinity; the big bright hall, jam packed with every type imaginable; students in duffel coats, punks in bin liners, shoe gazing youths, skinheads, hippies; They all had one thing in common; an absolute NEED to be in that hall and nowhere else on the planet that night, like Richard Dryfuss getting to the mountain in *Close Encounters* they simply had to be there.

As my girlfriend and I walked up the steps, out of a dark wet night, into the entrance foyer, the atmosphere hit me; there was a faint light, figures milling around, talking, shouting, drinking, smoking. The muffled sound from the main hall suddenly amplified when the inner doors were opened. All my senses were invaded; a kaleidoscope of colour, sound, and smell; that nauseating smell of dope. There was an earsplitting sound bouncing off the hard surfaces of the great hall. The room was unusually bright; there were large paintings of distinguished past alumni hanging from the walls. The ceiling was high and the air was hot and heavy.

The Count Bishops were the warm up act though I doubt if they signed up for the full and fiery onslaught they received from the crowd that night. At first I thought it was some kind of new lighting effect, a kind of arc from the stage to the front quarter of the crowd. We winced on realising the rainbow effect was caused by the continuous spitting from the crowd at the band. The moving arc, like arrows at Agincourt refracted through the beams of stage lights.

The 'Bishops fled, the hall darkened. The lull in hostilities followed by the rumble from the crowd announced the arrival of the new breed. Four men from the apocalypse took the stage. Bassist, Paul Simonon, wore a kind of black cobweb affair as he stood, legs akimbo. My girlfriend loved his spiky orange hair. Joe Strummer was like the little troublemaker in the middle; pent up, snarling, angry. Mick Jones did his odd 'running on the spot' thing. But it was Headon who captivated me that night. His sticks looked huge, he was also angry but he was in complete control, His drums gleamed and he played with the authority of a farrier at his anvil. The whole gig just seemed to hang on his solid sound. I have never seen a better drummer. EVER.

 I can't really remember the individual songs, a lot of *'1,2,3,4's'*…. followed by a wall of sound. The details don't matter because it was eye openingly, jaw droppingly, heart beatingly beautiful. I remember thinking to myself; THIS IS THE FUTURE.

How many bands were born that night? How many futures were changed?

By the end of the night, the atmosphere, the heat, the noise, the heaving, the pushing, and that smell of dope became too overpowering, and so it was I carried my collapsed girlfriend out to the foyer to get some fresh air. Years later in the T.V. Club dressing room, I mentioned this to Paul and he laughed out loud and said he was also at that gig. He too had ended up carrying his brother Larry (future guitarist of The Blades) out of the gig after he had become tired and emotional.

How many bands indeed!

17.

JOHN FISHER
(PROMOTER, THE DANDELION MARKET)
THE CLASH
DUBLIN, 1977

The Clash (and the dead cow's eye)

In October 1977, The Clash played two gigs in Trinity College in Dublin. It was the first 'Major League' punk gig here and at that point, I had been selling badges, t-shirts, posters etc. in the Dandelion Market for about four months. The punk scene was growing and myself and my partner were happy to be in the heart of the action and making a few bob as well.

When The Clash gigs were announced, we decided that we'd try to sell badges outside Trinity to fans going in and out of the gigs.

As the first fans were arriving, I spotted several of The Black Catholics appearing beside me. They were already notorious for starting fights and generally causing bother and I watched carefully as they started trying to relieve me of a few badges when they could. I knew what they were at and it ended up where they bought a few and nicked a few so we were all happy enough. One of them had a strange long blob swinging from a safety pin on his jacket. It looked interesting so I asked him what it was. In explanation, he squeezed one end of it and from the other end, a cow's dead eye appeared from its meaty socket! Lovely!

When all the fans were inside for the first show, myself and my friend wondered what to do until they re-emerged and the second wave of fans arrived. I knew where the Stage Door was and I reckoned that if we were lucky, we might be allowed leave our badge boards there while we went off for a while. So I knocked on the door and it was immediately opened by a face I immediately recognised - Joe Strummer. Without waiting, he said "Get in boys, quickly". I was suddenly painfully aware that our boards were full of 'unofficial' badges that they weren't going to be seeing a penny from and I quickly turned them away from the band who had all just appeared beside him. Joe didn't even look at the badges and just said "Right, we're heading onto the stage now so grab a couple of beers from the dressing room and come into the hall when you're ready". I couldn't believe our luck and we did just as he said. I ended up watching the gig from a great spot near the stage with a beer in my hand!

The sound was huge. The drums seemed to hit deep into the body and the bass shook through you. The guitars jangled into the head and the vocals screamed in your ears. A full-frontal assault on the body and soul.

Most people, even if too young to remember it, have heard stories about the gobbing at punk gigs. But maybe what doesn't get remembered was the full extent of it. The band were subjected to wave after wave of full-on torrents of the stuff that ended up dripping off their faces, guitars and even being swallowed, particularly by Joe Strummer. At one point, I suddenly noticed this projectile heading towards the stage. I recognized it immediately - the cow's eye I'd seen earlier. It landed somewhere in front of the stage and was hurtled back by whoever found it.

Later, as we were all filing out of the hall, I looked down at the rubbish strewn on the floor. And what did I see? Squashed, broken but still recognisable, that same cow's eye. Maybe it was symbolic of something profound but what exactly, I don't know or care. But I do know that I had just witnessed one of the best bands ever playing one of the best shows ever – and that I never want to see a dead cow's eye up close again.

18.

ELVERA BUTLER
(PROMOTER, HEAD OF REEKUS RECORDS)
FROM THE WHO TO THE STRANGLERS

I've been lucky to catch so many terrific gigs over the years, that it really is difficult to pick just one, whether it was my first experience of a big open air gig with The Who, complete with all the original members, at the Oval in the early '70s, supported by Rod Stewart and The Faces, and America, or Pink Flyod in Earls Court launching *Dark Side of the Moon'* and; that gig was a very different from any I'd been at before, a surreal, all embracing experience, with all sorts of technical wizardry such as surround sound and exploding planes that went right over the audience, so that wherever you were in the venue you were very much part of the experience. And in those pre-lazar days, they continued the magic with a light show outside the venue after the show, provided by army using search lights to ease the transition back to reality as we made our way to the tube station. An ardent fan, I saw them them again at Knebworth, and over the years in their different guises, from David Gilmour's Division Bell at Wembley in the mid '80s., to the much more magical Roger Waters' *'Dark Side of the Moon'* at the more intimate Marquee in Cork, and Roger Waters' *'The Wall'* in more recent years.

Dr Feelgood in the Hammersmith Odeon in '75 or '76 was a revelation too, in a very different way, with the anarchic chemistry between Wilco Johnson and Lee Brilleaux. While I had both play my venue, The Downtown Kampus in Cork, in their separate line-ups, the magic wasn't the same - interplay between the two and had created something way more than the sum of the parts.

My first big gig was Led Zeppelin in the Stadium in Dublin in '71, and I had a seat just over the stage so had a great view. A standout moment in my memory was Robert Plant sitting front of stage as he begun *'Stairway To Heaven'*, which they were trying out for Zeppelin IV. The atmosphere was brilliant, and the crowd just didn't want to let the band go – and they were happy to oblige, playing several encores.

And then there are the other elements that make a gig extra memorable, such as being responsible for the production and seeing the gig goes safely. The Stranglers in City Hall stands out as one of very heightened tension; it was 1977 and the band were at the height of their popularity. They exuded an air of menace, and the tension cranked up as the gig progressed where the audience were getting totally unmanageable with excitement and things could tip over into complete anarchy at any moment, but ultimately held together – those moments are pretty special. Speaking to Hugh Cornwell in recent years, he remembered the gig well, and was surprised at how well they were known in Cork, as they had thought of it as some strange outpost on the fringes of Europe – this was prior to The Downtown Kampus gig, and Cork becoming a regular part of touring Ireland, along with Belfast and Dublin.

So what makes a gig memorable or special? I've seen artists perform that I had revered for years and had lived and loved with every album recorded, who so disappointed by their lack lustre live performance that it took years before I could re-capture the magic of listening to those pre-loved albums. And others who had not necessarily been listened to much on record who created such a riveting live show.

And sometimes it seems it's a case of 'you had to be there'.

19.

BRIAN SEALES
DC NIEN, TOKYO OLYMPICS)
THE STRANGLERS
DUBLIN, 1978

April 2013. Nerves are building up. I sat in the iconic Exam Hall of Trinity College Dublin waiting for the commencement of the first exam of my final year of a science degree. As I gaze around the hall I realise I was here once before in Nov 1977, to see The Stranglers on what may have been their first visit to Dublin at the height of the punk rock era. What a night that was. Everyone packed in like sardines, a strange mix of spikey haired punks and hippies with long hair and beards, but all sharing sweat and atmosphere. I was one of those hippies at the time and The Stranglers were like a breath of fresh air on the music scene when I first heard them.

The gig was stunning even if the sound was terrible. Just the sheer energy of the band was enough to make the crowd heave, hop, pogo, whatever it was we all did back then. And… the heat, I remember that. Hugh Cornwall didn't like being spat on, who would, and threatened to call off the gig. Jean Jacques belted some punk with his bass guitar after the guy spat at him. He probably showed his bruises off with pride later that night "Jean Jacques did this to me….." However the band won me over, like The Doors on speed, I remember thinking. I also remember thinking "I can do this". So, at twenty years of age, all study was dropped, a band was formed with some friends and off we went. DC Nien was born and although never reaching the lofty heights which the Stranglers achieved over the years at least I had tried and went on to experience much the same as The Stranglers had on that night in 1977. I was brought back to reality by an announcement…."You May Start. The Exam has begun". My nerves were gone, thinking of the Stranglers and that gig. I was probably the only person in the exam hall who was smiling while reading the exam questions. A tune was running through my head "Whatever happened to? All the heroes"………….

20.

BARRY COOKE
(DEAD FRIDGE IN THE ROAD)
STIFF LITTLE FINGERS
DUBLIN, 1978

It all started on a dark almost winters night in a pub in Donnybrook with a bunch of under-age lads drinking a pint and two. Emmett said he heard there was a punk band playing in UCD. So we all trekked up to some big dark hall in Belfield, shivering in the unheated hall.

The band were late and the gig nearly didn't go ahead as the PA was never delivered. So the band I never heard of, Stiff Little Fingers, played with just their guitar amps turned up full. The passion they played their music with in front of less than 100 people in a dark cold hall was worthy of the accolade I give them here. They managed to fill the huge hall with incredible sound and passion. Their words and music are still as relevant today as 1978.

21.

PAUL CHARLES
(BOOKING AGENT, ASGARD AGENCY, AUTHOR, THE LONESOME HEART IS ANGRY)
SIGNING THE UNDERTONES
BELFAST, 1978

Sometime in the late summer of 1978 a friend in Belfast sent me a copy of a locally released e.p. Naturally enough it was vinyl record with a fold around jacket. I remember it arrived on a Friday and I played it a few times in the office that afternoon and took it home and played it for the entire weekend; first to convince myself what I was hearing was as brilliant as I initially thought and then purely for the sheer enjoyment. The more I played the e.p. the more I couldn't believe that it was written, recorded and released on a small Northern Irish independent label. To my ears the title song was a world-beating classic. I was convinced that when it was released in the world in general, and Europe and the USA, in particular, it was going to shoot straight to the top of the charts and stay there forever.

The e.p. featured the following songs: 'True Confessions', 'Smarter Than U' and 'Emergency Cases' - all brilliant sub-two-minute originals - plus, of course, the legendary 'Teenage Kicks', which, while clocking in at 2 minutes and 38 seconds, was the longest song and also the title of the e.p. The local label was Terri Hooley's Good Vibrations (later it was re-released on Sire Records.) 'Teenage Kicks' was written by Northern Ireland's other great songwriter, John O'Neill.

The band I'm referring to is The Undertones!

I tracked them down and met up with them later when I was in Belfast for a few Van Morrison concerts. We chatted for ages; they definitely gave off a very positive all-for-one and one-for-all vital band vibe and shared their own unique brand of band humour. They told jokes mostly at each other expense and I tried to explain to them how my side (live gigs) of the music business worked. They proved that underneath the humour they'd been listening closely to what I was saying as, time after time, they'd ask the correct questions. The Undertones agreed to come to Asgard for their live work as long as they were allowed to do it their way and we would tailor the touring so that they were never away from Derry for too long. So strong was their independent stance - even at that early stage - that they clearly didn't want to sell themselves short for the price of a cup of tea and a cheese (or egg) sandwich by insisting on buying their own.

Clearly a legion of people loved Teenage Kicks just as much as I did, but it never achieved the chart success it deserved, proving the point that in the music business, being brilliant isn't always enough. However over the next five years they played some of the best live shows I have ever witnessed.

22.

GERRY SMYTH
(AUTHOR NOISY ISLAND: A SHORT HISTORY OF IRISH POPULAR MUSIC)
THE BOOMTOWN RATS
DUBLIN, 1978

I was sixteen at the time, and fully committed to the revolution that had (as I thought) convulsed popular music over the previous two years.

There was plenty of 'punk' action around the city, but the 'Rats were something else. They had a London deal, and they had appeared on the British weekly popular music show *Top of the Pops*, which even for (most) new wave bands was still the *sine qua non* for success.

The album *'Tonic for the Troops'* had appeared in June, spawning three high octane pop-punk singles: 'She's So Modern', *'Like Clockwork'* and the mini opera *'Rat Trap'*. The latter would become the Rats' first number one in November, and was especially thrilling because of its apparent Dublin setting.

Punk created a moral panic throughout the UK, and was even more feared and demonised in holy Catholic Ireland. The 'Rats wanted to play their home town but couldn't find a venue willing to book them, until the Olympia – a beautiful old Victorian music hall and theatre specialising in light popular entertainment – agreed to run the gig. What were they thinking?!

Originally built in 1879, the Olympia had hosted some of the most famous names in entertainment history – people such as Charlie Chaplin, Laurel and Hardy, Noel Coward, Alec Guinness, Edith Evans and Marcel Marceau. The theatre had survived redesign, war, revolution, demolition orders and (in 1974) literal collapse. But was it ready for the 'Rats?

I'd been to a few gigs already, most memorably at the Stadium on the South Circular Road where I'd seen acts such as Horslips, J.J. Cale and the Flying Burrito Brothers. But seeing one of the hottest new bands on the block at a Dublin city-centre venue which was not really geared up for it remains one of the most compelling experiences of my youth.

Our crowd bussed in from Firhouse, seven miles to the south, expectations revved up to fever pitch by a few flagons of cider earlier in the evening. Dame Street was electric, with hundreds of teenagers milling around in an atmosphere of tense excitement.

When we eventually got in, the venue seemed somewhat at odds with the frankly threatening atmosphere on the street outside. The auditorium was full of seats, with nowhere to stand or dance. How was this going to work?

Well, to use the rock 'n' roll parlance, we wrecked the joint. As soon as Geldof appeared people at the front stood up, and as soon as that happened, people behind them began standing on the seats, and as soon as that happened, other people behind *them* started standing on the backs of seats, balanced precariously between rows. The place began to bounce and the seats began to break. The poor staff tried to get people to sit down again, but it was like trying to herd cats (or rats).

I don't know how much damage was done to the Olympia that night, and I don't remember much about the details of the gig (I think the Vipers supported?). What lives in my mind chiefly is a vague impression of energy, freedom, recklessness and youth unbounded – that heady cocktail of emotions and effects that continues to make rock 'n' roll and its derivatives such a powerful social force.

23.

PAT O'DONNELL
(THE FOUNTAINHEAD, PRODUCER)
IAN DURY AND THE BLOCKHEADS
DUBLIN, 1978

Dublin was great in the late 1970's. The music, the venues and the people.

Having spent my early days listening to Pink Floyd and Led Zeppelin and coming from Dun Laoghaire, it was time to shed my hippy skin!

Something new was happening in music and it was exciting.

The Olympic ballroom had the faded glory of old dance halls (just like the TV Club around the corner in Harcourt Street) but it was now hosting punk and new wave acts from the UK. So, my pal Gary and I went to see Ian Dury and the Blockheads who had released the album "New Boots and Panties" the previous year.

What a gig! What an incredible band! Amazing brass section, infectious funk punk grooves, and the man himself. A great performer, with an incredible stage presence the likes of which I'd never seen before. We were mesmerized by this new shift in music and the promise it brought.

'Wake Up And Make Love With Me', *'Billericay Dickie'* and *'Hit Me With Your Rhythm Stick'*, all songs to remember.

There have been many gigs since and hopefully many more to come, but this one just stayed with me. Such energy, hope and spirit. Just what you want from a great gig.

24.

RAYMOND GORMAN
(THAT PETROL EMOTION, EVERLASTING YEAH)
DEXY'S MIDNIGHT RUNNERS
COLERAINE, 1979

Dexy's Midnight Runners played our backwater college (the New University of Ulster in Coleraine, N. Ireland) on March 6 1979. It remains the greatest gig that I have ever seen to this day. At the time the band were relatively unknown and had only released one 45, the magnificent *'Dance Stance'*. My friends and I had a copy of course and when we heard that they were coming to play we were gibbering wrecks. This was a BIG deal. For a band of their calibre to be making the trip across the water as the Troubles rumbled on was unheard of. Singer and main man Kevin Rowland was of Irish heritage all the same. He possessed the questing, fearless spirit of the "fíor gael". We told everyone that this was a show not to be missed but in typical fashion few listened and on the night the crowd consisted of maybe fifty people at most. The low attendance mattered not a jot. When they finally swaggered on stage in their Mean Streets garb the band didn't even seem to notice. With just one song they blew the place apart and all the tiny minds therein. People were just staring at them open mouthed, incredulous at what they were witnessing and hearing – song after fantastic song of this empowering, majestic noise that lifted up your very soul. The fifty roared their approval. Band and audience felt invincible. They played like there was 50,000 present. The intensity of the delivery was staggering. The horn players, guitarist, and bassist would at key moments synchronise and move forward putting their feet up on the monitors for dramatic effect. They would all look heroically skyward as if they were serenading the Goddess Herself. It was definitely a religious experience for all those who saw the show. We talked of little else for months afterwards. It defined our young lives and inspired me to become a musician. Eight weeks later *'Geno'* was released and went to number one in the UK charts.

25.

DAVID LINEHAN
(AIDAN WALSH AND THE SCREAMING EAGLES, HOOLIGAN)

It's hard to pick just one favourite gig so here a few that stand out for me:

ROCKY DEVALERA & THE GRAVEDIGGERS
THE DANDELION MARKET, SAT 28TH APRIL 1979

The first gig I was ever at. Punk / punk influenced music was still very fresh and exciting and the Dandelion was a scene with a real vibe to it. You had a sense that literally anything could -and indeed did- happen...I have a vague memory of loud Dr. Feelgood type R&B music played by men clad in black, it might have been atrocious but 10 year old me loved it! The gig is further fixed in my mind by the fact that we gained entrance to the venue via a hole in the side wall... it was a badge of honour in those days to get into a gig without paying!

NAPALM SUNDAY
BASE X... A SATURDAY AFTERNOON GIG AROUND 1981

The pokey dimly lit "Basement", a record shop on Bachelors Walk, was crammed wall to wall with punks. It had no stage just the band set up in one corner outside the counter. The atmosphere was highly charged, audience members would have been clutching two-litres of cider and I remember getting the pungent smell of hash. Napalm Sunday were in their ascension, there was a sense that they were our own and that after so many "poseur" bands, here at last was the genuine article. They had the songs, the power and a sense of purpose about them.

SEARCH & DESTROY, THE GREEN, POWERSTORM
THE DAME TAVERN, MARCH 1987

The first gig I played. We were 3rd on the bill playing to a packed upstairs room, made up 99% of punks from town. Our set comprised of four originals and one cover. Harry Callaghan (RIP) our singer, a figurehead of the Dublin punk scene, had got there before the rest of us and had drank 10 pints of Guinness before we got on stage. It was my job to let him know when to come in for each verse and each chorus...needless to say it didn't go to plan!

AIDAN WALSH & THE SCREAMING EAGLES
THE CATHEDRAL CLUB – SUMMER 1988

Aidan's big album launch gig featuring the Golden Horde, Something Happens, Kill Devil Hill and a host of Dublin's most popular indie bands of the day. Highly enjoyable but absolutely terrifying as we were headlining and it was only the second gig in any band that we'd ever played!

ANGELIC UPSTARTS
THE TEMPODROME BERLIN, SEPTEMBER 1989

My second gig with the 'Upstarts and first time to go to continental Europe with a band. We'd played to 7-800 in a squatted club in Hamburg the night before but this was on a completely different scale; headlining an anti-fascist festival to 7,000 people, just a couple of weeks before the Berlin wall came down.... heady times!

26.

RORY STOKES
(THE SUSSED, THE SPIDERS FROM KIMMAGE)
BEST MEMORIES OF THE SUSSED!

The Sussed supported U2 numerous times:

1979: I was age 14 - we supported them in Howth Community Centre. We brought all our gear except the Bass drum (wouldn't fit on Bus) on two buses to Howth. Larry Mullen said we couldn't borrow his so we hiked across Howth Hill and back to borrow one off Neil McCormack (Hot Press & U2 biographer).

We played a cover of Radiators From Space *'Television Screen'* that night & were mortified to come off stage & see the late Phil Chevron for The Radiators in the crowd (turned out he liked it).

1980: Age 15 - The Sussed supported U2 in Dandelion Market! Entry fee was 50p. We really enjoyed ourselves and went down well. During U2's set Bono (wearing black String Vest & Chessboard Trousers) dragged me up on stage during the song *'Boy/Girl'* from their first single & stripped me from the waist up. I think I was supposed to represent The Boy on their first album cover. This continued for quite a while until a very cold night in UCD & he tried it and I had buttoned up my shirt & jumper all the way against the cold and was left spread-eagled on the stage for five minutes until I got my inside out clothes unbuttoned.

1981: I was age 15 - The Sussed first single, *'Don't Swim On The East Coast'*, (which was about Windscale (now called Sellafield), reached number three in the Irish Charts Larry Gogan had it his Record of the Week & Dave Fanning played it every night for ages.

The Sussed were famous for their graffiti and 'That Poster'

The Graffiti started out as street signs & then down the back of buses. I and fans utilised the BLACK MARKER which instead of being used on single buses were taken to bus depots across Dublin where The Sussed was written upstairs at the front so everyone could see for their entire journey!

Many fans also wrote the name on the back of toilet doors of ferries and planes as far away as Bahrain. I also wrote The Sussed on every IR£Pounds notes I came across & was most surprised one night in Bartley Dunnes pub to get a note back in my change with 'The Sussed written on it, but not in my handwriting

That Poster : The Rolling Stones were rumoured to be coming to Dublin.

The Sussed capitalised by printing a thousand dayglow green huge posters with The Sussed as Support act to the Stones in Leixlip Castle on June 31st - pasted them ALL OVER Dublin

Every single newspaper had it on their front page.

Not one bar Niall Stokes Hot Press realised that there was no June 31st!!!!!

Loads of free publicity.

The Sussed are on YouTube, www.facebook.com/thesussed & www.myspace.com/thesussed where you can watch Videos & tonnes of Photos. The Sussed are currently in the studio recording old and a few new songs using 21st century tech – Watch this space!!!!!!!!

27.

FRANK RYNNE
(THOSE HANDSOME DEVILS, THE BABYSNAKES)
THE RAMONES
DUBLIN, 1980

In 1980 I was brought by my three older brothers to see the Ramones at the State Cinema in Phibsborough. I was 14 but the Ramones were form favourite band form when I was 11 and my brother John came back from college at Christmas with the first Ramones and Stranglers LPs. I would sit outside my elder brothers bedroom listening to the bizarre music that broke with their Bowie obsession. Beat on the Brat with a baseball bat was what hooked me.

No music had lyrics like that and as a child of 11 they enflamed me.

Getting to the gig was like a march of death. On all the garden and walls and lining the streets were skinheads intent on violence and the punks or punters walked in tight packs towards the venue. Inside there was seating which seemed inappropriate. Big bouncers put people in their seats and the anticipation grew, I can't remember who supported but on the first an Un Du Tree Faw uttered by Dee Dee Ramone the seated mass ran forward to occupy the first ten rows literally pogoing on the seats until they collapsed and bits of cast iron and cushion were passed forward to the pit.

The intensity of the performance was total. Band as machine. Bouncers just gave up. The venue trashed. Johnny and Dee Dee flaying the audience with intensity and showering with plectrums in the micro seconds between songs. I got one, Dee Dee's. Joey a singular stoical beanpole, without any of the excess movement of other stars.

After the show there were four stabbings, the skins being still active. I cringed at the next day's Press and Herald as I was sure I would never get parental permission to see a show again.

The remarkable scene inside the venue had been one of calm self help, it seemed incredulous that outside on the street idiots would target lone punks with knives.

I saw Ramones a dozen times after and in 1985 or 6 got their autographs on my copies of 'It's Alive' and 'Leave Home' and spent a late night with Joey and Marky in Blooms Hotel.

Hey Ho! Let's Go!

28.

BILLY MCGRATH
(UCD ENTS OFFICER 1975-1976, MANAGER OF THE ATRIX AND STAGALEE, TV PRODUCER, DOCUMENTARY MAKER)
U2
LONDON, 1980

Not so much as the best gig of my life but more an appreciation of the best live band in the world. And they grew up under my nose! I will get to U2 Live in Modena Italy in due course but nobody has ever asked me to write about best ever live gigs before so if you have a few minutes join me on a wee journey beforehand.

We all have all opinions of U2 and I suppose with me once sharing a house with Sir Bob and co-organising Ireland's first ever national rock tour; managing Ireland's No.1 live band Stagalee (Hot Press 1978) and later much loved The Atrix, I had an eye and ear behind the scenes of the Irish rock scene. I saw the four-piece from Dublin's northside develop over the years differently than most. From The Dandelion to McGonagles, TV Club to the National Stadium. I turned down a chance to book out the band as agent in Ireland – and before Bono and Adam left my flat and got the bus back into town I threw them an idea to turn their June residency in McGonagles into Xmas shows. That's another story.

My true appreciation of that was going with this 4 piece started in 1980.

In March I organised the rock section of The Sense of Ireland in London. U2 and The Atrix were two of the acts. Both played different venues. As U2 didn't have a lighting person their manager (& friend) Paul McGuinness saw what I was doing with The Atrix and asked me would I do the honours. So now I had a job to do. With such a small lighting system and say 8 or 10 lamps you have to be as varied as you can. During the show I never realised how much I knew/liked the songs and how 'visual' the music was. The band took the packed small crowd by the scruff of its neck and afterwards back at the 'team' hotel Paul & the band agreed their contract with Island Records. Of course it was the 'lightshow'. And Paul still owes me the tenner he promised (STERLING!) – but that's another story.

Later I ran the PR side of their brilliant homecoming show at the Phoenix Park and running in and out of radio, press and TV interviews it was good to get to spend time with them as people. They are a grounded and solid interesting group of individuals. Couple of years later I joined RTE as a producer / director with music top of the list. Our paths crossed again. U2 were generous enough to allow me to produce & direct two TV docs – one in 1985 based around their Croke Park sold out show and the second a couple of years later – a half hour special from their live show from Modena near Bologna in Italy. The first was a one off mad filming challenge and I probably caught the band for a couple of songs. Dave Fanning was the host of the shorter Italian film and it was part of an 8 part series Visual Eyes.

If you ever see the '*U2 Live In Modena*' half hour on You Tube you can see that the show included less than a minute of the band live. That is because we were told the camera lead had to be unplugged after the first 50 seconds of the band walking on stage at the packed heaving football stadium. After the show at the backstage bar I think I had my first ever and last row with Paul McGuinness why we had we were denied some decent live footage.

Now I understand what he was doing – and the protection of image rights is everywhere now - but all I was fighting for was the fact that we had travelled so far and felt short changed. I was thinking of the RTE viewer! That night and row was actually the reason I left RTE two years later to join a Channel 4 music series but that's another story! We filmed by day before the two shows and had to turn the camera off for the full set minus 50 seconds on both nights so we shot side stage on the first night and from the middle of the football stadium at the sound desk on night 2. It was there I was hit by the lightbulb moment!

I sat there behind audio wizard Joe O'Herlihy on a flycase and sucked a beer in the warm evening. Over the next 2 hours I twigged that I was watching the Best Live Band in the World.

That impact and emotion has never stopped. Over the years the venues & songs may change but the band remains the same. Not many bands stick together or members survive for forty years? There is something special about seeing the same four guys you saw let's face it as kids stay the course and then to go on and rewrite the rules of the industry and the road. I am a fan and U2 live always reminds me why I love live music so much. I must get out more. That thought occurred to me as I listened to U2's new album driving up and down to Donegal in summer 2015. It is very very good and I suddenly got the goo to hear the songs live.

So at 7.30pm on November 10th 2015 I was at the Bercy Stadium in Paris waiting for the houselights to dim as 4 men from Dublin take the stage. I definitely was not alone.

But that's another story.

29.

SÉAN O'CONNOR
(THE LOOKALIKES)
THIN LIZZY, THE LOOKALIKES
DUBLIN, 1980

I have many memorable and pleasant memories from my musical career, from the legends of the music industry I've been fortunate to play with, to playing to major crowds including 77,000 football fans in Soldiers Field, Chicago, before a Bears game. Aside from the incredible buzz and audience attendance and reaction to our regular gigs in Dublin on a weekly basis, two things stand out as highlights for me personally and The Lookalikes in general.

Both were when we supported Thin Lizzy on the U.K. and Ireland tour in 1980. The first was when Philip asked me backstage at the De Montford Hall in Leicester if I would like to play lead guitar on the encores with Lizzy that night. I played *'The Rocker'* and *'Whiskey In The Jar'*, and the audience went crazy, as Thin Lizzy didn't play *'Whiskey In The Jar'* in their set normally. I guested with them many times after that, but the first time will always stay in my memory, as it was like a boyhood dream come true.

One of the best memories with The Lookalikes was when we came home to Ireland on the same tour and played the RDS in Dublin with Lizzy. We had a very big and loyal following at the gig, and I think it's fair to say we went down as well as Lizzy did, and we actually outsold them in merchandising! The atmosphere was electric when we were playing, and to stop singing and have 6,000 people singing our songs back to us is something I will happily take to my grave with me. They were great times indeed.

30.

PETER DEVLIN
(THE DEVLINS, PRODUCER, BROADCASTER)
THE SPECIALS AND THE BEAT
DUBLIN, 1981

This was the first and most exciting, inspirational and terrifying gig of my life. I bought my ticket in Golden Discs the day they went on sale but my friends were too late as it sold out almost immediately so I ended up going alone.

The venue was packed, I'm guessing the number exceeded the capacity which was, I think, 1,400. The opening act were The Beat who were so good they got an encore. Or was that just another interruption near the end of their set due to the sporadic outbreaks of violence at the front of the stage? Either way, they got an incredible reception from a crowd who were, at that time, starved of live performances by bands from outside Ireland.

As The Specials took to the stage there was an obvious air of nervous anticipation, excitement, tension and underlying hostility. When they played the opening song *'Concrete Jungle'* it all went off and seemed like everyone in the first ten rows began fighting.

The violence interrupted the show several times with lead singer Terry Hall repeatedly pleading with the crowd to calm down, but despite all of this, the show was sublime. Individually the Specials were great players who, combined, made up the most exciting band of the 2-Tone movement. Watching them play I forgot about the surroundings and concentrated on the music and it was this gig that made me want to get a guitar and form a band. The Specials had everything, a performance that was mesmerising to watch, music that made you dance and lyrics that made you think. Well, most people thought about the lyrics, the exception being the skinheads and punks at the front of the crowd that night. Not content with fighting among themselves, they invaded the stage, stole the microphones and toppled the p.a., bringing the gig to an abrupt end.

Exactly one month later in one of the worst disasters in the history of the state, a fire swept through the venue killing 48 people. The Stardust never re-opened after the tragedy.

31.

PAUL BYRNE
(IN TUA NUA, PRODUCER)
ECHO AND THE BUNNYMEN
DUBLIN, 1981

In 1980 there was a new and exciting music scene starting to emerge in Ireland as punk moved to the post punk and new romantic era. I was playing with 'Deaf Actor' at the time, a band that had started as a 'Doors' style rock outfit called 'Sounds Unreel' but had developed into a very experimental hard-edged post punk outfit. About this time a new agency opened up in Dublin called MCD. They were a two-man outfit with one guy in Belfast and one in Dublin. They seemed to have their finger on the pulse and were bringing in some great bands to smaller venues in Dublin. I managed to get one of their numbers, that of the young Denis Desmond, and from that moment on I plagued him for gigs. Eventually, in 1981, we hit the jackpot as Denis gave us two great support slots in the now legendary McGonagles. The first was to open for a Liverpool band called 'The Teardrop Explodes'. Fronted by the charismatic Julian Cope, they had just had a couple of hit singles and were a band on the up.

The second was for another Liverpool band, and our biggest influence at the time, Echo and The Bunnymen. They had just released their second album *'Heaven Up Here'* which had been heralded as an even bigger triumph than their first album *'Crocodiles'*. When we arrived in for the Bunnymen gig the band was still sound checking. I remember they were playing *'All My Colours'* or *'Zimbo'* as it would become better known as. The song featured a great backdrop of tom playing by their drummer Pete de Freitas and the sound coming through the PA was one of the best drum sounds I had ever heard. He was playing a black Tama five piece kit with the bottom heads removed from the toms and he hit the drums harder and with more attitude than anyone I had seen before. As soon as they left the stage we were told to get our gear on and do a quick sound-check.

As we played a couple of numbers I noticed Pete watching me, which of course made me completely self-conscious. When we stopped he came over to me with a big smile and started to talk about my kit and in particular my electronic drum or Pollard Syndrum as it was known. I used it for a big explosive sound to boost the odd snare hit. Pete told me that he had done the same when he recorded Zimbo but had wrecked his from hitting it too hard. Then he asked me if he could borrow it for their gig. That was probably my proudest moment to date as a drummer. Pete de Freitas was going to use MY syndrum.

We had a great time playing our 30-minute set to a packed house but my enduring memory was the thrill of watching Pete beat the shit out of my Syndrum. I also changed my approach to drumming that night and decided to hit the drums harder to try and make that clear sound from every hit that Pete was so good at.

Years later, in 1987, I was in Holland with In Tua Nua playing at the Pink Pop festival. We were on in the afternoon (in the lashing rain) and The Bunnymen were headlining that night. All day long I had strolled up the steps onto the side of the stage to watch other bands with no problem but the band I really wanted to see up close, and in particular the drummer, was the Bunnymen. As I arrived at the steps there was a security guy telling everyone that only the band's guests would be allowed up. At this I nipped around the back of the stage before I was corralled and moved on with the rest of the crowd that had assembled. I figured if I waited for a few songs I might get lucky with a second attempt. As I hung around behind the massive outdoor stage someone started to pull open the tarp which closes off the back of the stage. To my amazement Pete de Freitas emerged undoing his fly for a quick pee before his gig (obviously one too many beers in the dressing room). Just as before he greeted me with a big smile and we got chatting. I told him the story about McGonagles and he politely pretended to remember the gig and the Syndrum. When he discovered why I was hiding out he told me to hop up and he brought me in to watch from behind the kit, which is the only way to really see what a drummer is doing. Once again I saw the passion and determination with which he played even when using brushes on some of the newer numbers like *'Ocean Rain'*. After the gig Pete came over to me to say goodbye and then vanished in the post gig entourage. On other occasions I would get to sit behind Larry Mullen (U2) and Mel Gaynor (Simple Minds) to watch their technique also.

In 1989, I spent 4 months in LA writing and recording In Tua Nua's last album. I was in the smaller group sent out to do some advance work on the songs before the studio sessions began. Of course we found a great little bar near our apartment to hang out in when we weren't busy and the barman turned out to be my old pal Mark Shepherd, the drummer from Dublin band 'Light A Big Fire'. We spent plenty of evenings and sometimes afternoons in there with Mark and our new friend Bonnie Stern. On June 14th 1989 I walked in to the bar and Mark called me over looking very grim. He asked had I heard the news about Pete de Freitas. I had not. Pete had died from a head on collision while riding his high-powered motorbike in England. He was only 27.

RIP Pete de Freitas.

32.

ANDREW BASS
(REVEILLE, STUDIO OWNER, PRODUCER)
U2, REVEILLE
GALWAY, 1981

It was November 1981 and I was sweet sixteen. Well only as sweet as a strict diet of The Clash, Talking Heads, The Stranglers, The Jam, Pistols and XTC etc would allow. So, sixteen and pretty angst ridden, and full of foreboding for the Leaving. Certain that I would monumentally fail.... but not sweetly.

The phone rang in the hallway of the middle class house where I lived with my brothers and misled parents (all parents have been misled by a capitalist society when you're 16). The stranger on the other end of the line asked for me, which in itself was rather odd as I was seldom allowed use the phone due to prank calling Mrs Sinclair across the road - which was great fun. The caller explained he was Larry from the pop group U2 and had been to our gig in Mount Temple School (he had just left Mount Temple the previous year) and would we like us to support his band in Galway in June of the following year.

Although nowhere near the echelons of their current status U2 were tipped as 'just as good as The Blades and The Lookalikes'. I told him to fuck off believing him to be my piss taking friend Kevin.

The previous week I had rented a PA system from Pat Dolans and borrowed amplifiers from mates in order for my band to perform in the school Gym after some ceremony or other. Steve Bass, my brother was playing erm... bass, Dave Horner (later to be a member of the fantastic 'Furious Colour' and less fantastic 'Black Velvet Band') was bashing the drums. I owned a copy Telecaster and twanged punky poppy riffs utilising all three chords I knew in the wrong order and wailing utter rubbish into the mic. I was the singer now as I'd fired our vocalist because she wrote a song called *'Monkey In A Cage'*, which in retrospect was a better title than any I came up with in '81 (with the exception of *'Suicide Sue'* but more of that later). We called ourselves Reveille.

So, after I told Larry to fuck off, he rang me back and convinced me he was indeed the drummer with U2 and not the mischievous Kevin I thought him to be. He explained that they'd just released the *'October'* album, would be touring it in the new year and would be pleased to have us as support band in Galway at the Leisureland complex in Salthill. I might have had an erection, not because I'm sexually attracted to any member of U2 but because I was 16 and anything good (and bad) might arouse me.

My dad said no initially due to the gig happening just prior to the leaving cert, but relented on account of my impending and inevitable doom as a scholar. Even the great Protestant work ethic knows when to quit.

We rehearsed in the school (ironically in the same room that U2 used to use). Note: It's a testimony to the tutors and ethos of Mount Temple who were just as concerned about so called 'extra curricular' activities as academic studies. Indeed, Donald Moxham, my year head, was the man who encouraged U2 and sorted rehearsal space for many bands. It was also he who brought young Mullen to our gig (and probably asked him to ring me).

I asked Larry for a few quid to cover expenses. He told me, with a smile, that support bands don't get paid but he'd see what he could do. I think thirty pounds was offered to cover the cost of van driver.

I asked Ivan Mc Cormack (guitar player with 'Yeah Yeah' at the time and whose brother later wrote 'Killing Bono') would he bring us to the gig for a small consideration.....the aforementioned £30. He agreed and we were ready to roll.

The band, girlfriends and Ivan set off for Salthill. I was completely convinced I'd be discovered at the gig considering one of my mates told me I was quite good.....and I had almost mastered minor chords (wasn't sure at the time what being discovered meant but reckoned it probably offered the chance to dodge a 'normal job').

We arrived for sound check and observed two juggernauts parked at the venue. We gingerly squeezed the rented Hiace van in between them. I think the panic set in at the sight of the huge PA (I was only used to Pat Dolans 100 watt systems, this was slightly larger) the massive space for the great unwashed and the many laminate wearing personnel busying themselves with important giggy jobs. I walked into the venue trying to take in all in whilst holding my girlfriends hand. Turned out it wasn't my girlfriends hand: in the confusion both myself and Dave had interlocked fingers believing each other to be our girlfriends. An embarrassing defumble ensued and we endeavoured to compose ourselves and swagger across the expanse of the massive hall, like normal rock stars.

This was not a good start to the gig where I would be discovered.

There's something about sound checking a bass drum with a large production. You know that feeling when the low end nearly knocks you over? Well, I've had it ever since. For a million sound checks since (possible exaggeration here) I can feel that tinge of excitement, anticipation and rush to the head once a sound check has begun and the show is under way. Anyhoo, I think that's the first time I felt it. It's a drug.

To check the vocals Bono sang *'Gloria'* on his tod. Nuff said. The rest of their sound check eludes me.

Then there was disastrous news. The other support band, with the best moniker ever 'Some Kind Of Wonderful' had broken down and couldn't make the gig. We were supposed to use their gear. Larry stepped in and said we could use U2's gear, which at the time I figured was normal, because I was a 16 year old knob.

The Edge offered to help me set up and kindly asked if I'd like a clean or dirty sound. Having no idea what either meant I asked him if he'd ever heard The Blades. He said he was familiar with them. I asked if he could make me sound like Paul Cleary. Seemingly both bands had a competitive vibe at the time.

We chugged through a tune during sound check with an audience of just U2 who clapped mannerly when we finished. Not sure what happened between sound check and gig but I distinctly remember the stairway from the rear of the building to the stage. I must have run up and down it a dozen times, such was the adrenalin flowing through my teenage body (I think our maximum audience at that stage was about 20 or 30 relations, Here was a full house of over 1,000 unknown peeps).

I ran across the huge stage, telecaster in hand, plugged into Edge's AC30 and started the first song. When the band didn't come in at the right time I turned around to observe Dave clambering up the drum riser and Steve searching for the bass rig input (from a great distance). Eight bars later they joined me in the epic *'Suicide Sue'*, which we'd written the week before and would later sell a million copies.......not.

Later in the gig, I turned around and observed that someone had switched on Larry's fan behind the kit and Dave's hair was basically blowing vertically across his face. He copped me having a snigger at his expense and gave me the two finger salute. Nobody discovered me at the gig. I'm not going to mention the U2 gig. Only an idiot would believe that they weren't destined for greatness if they saw them play live.

We stayed over in Galway and in the morning wandered over to the amusement arcades in Salthill. Knowing that I was the coolest thing around (having fronted my band as support to U2 without shitting my pants during the gig), I posed at the pinball machine (mainly because there's a pic of Joe Strummer playing pinball on the *'London Calling'* album). A teenage girl broke away from her group and tentatively asked me if I was the singer of the band that played before U2 last night. Yes, I replied, did you enjoy the show? Wasn't there myself, she said, but all my mates over there said you were shite.

33.

CÁIT O'RIORDAN
(THE POGUES, RADIATORS, PRENUP)
U2
1981

Having reached middle age, I find that I can remember gigs I went to in the early 1980s, and I can remember gigs I went to this year. The intervening decades are just a blur. From those first few years my best memory is of seeing U2 play the Lyceum, London in 1981. I was a huge fan at the time, I knew every moment of their first two LPs by heart, and they were my favourite band in the world. At the time they were touring 'October', their second album. I was sad to read, years later, that it's the band's least favourite album, as it was my favourite and it was a thrill and an education to see those guys create the sounds I knew from the LP live, on stage, right in front of us. I smile now to think how amazed I was when Edge played piano, or that his harmonies matched Bono so well. The other vital factor of that gig was the U2 audience, people who, just like me, knew all the words, loved the band, and were delighted to be there. At the end of the show, rather than shouting for encores, the entire audience starting singing 'Rejoice'. The house lights came up, the side doors of the old theatre were opened and we spilled out into The Strand. It was cold and clear, the Christmas lights were blazing, and hundreds and hundreds of happy young people drifted towards Charing Cross, singing together.

In March this year I went to Paris to check out Mark Lanegan playing a cool old place in the 10th arrondissement. Paris rock audiences would break your heart with their commitment to never breaking a sweat, but the place was packed and attentive. From his first song, it was clear that Lanegan's voice was blown and I thought the show was going to be a dud. But instead of retreating behind the vocal limitations and delivering a soft, cautious show, the damage and restriction seemed to bring out the teenage punk in him – he applied full power to every song and it all worked. It was a wild, raw, visceral performance and the bravest thing I've ever seen a singer do.

34.

STANO
(ARTIST, MUSICIAN, COMPOSER)
TOM WAITS
DUBLIN, 1981

It's tough to pick one stand out gig, it's like trying to pick out a favourite album. Over the years I've seen some great gigs, the Clash, Stranglers, Henry Rollins, the Rollins gig because I never really liked his records, I thought they were too polished but when I saw his two gigs in the Tivoli I was really blown away, the second night was completely different to the first. He reacted and responded to his audience whereas a lot of bands you go to see use the same set and the same anecdotes at every gig in every city.

But my absolute favourite gig of all time was Tom Waits in the Olympia on the 27th March 1981 not only was it an amazing gig but it was my 21st birthday. I sat up in the Gods by myself as none of my friends were interested in going. What struck me about the gig was how the character and atmosphere of the building really added to the mood he created on stage. Even though I was as far from the stage as you could be, the power of his performance stretched all the way up to the Gods. The simplicity of one man and a piano telling stories.

There is one piece that stays with me to this day, as vivid as if it was yesterday, almost like a dream that you never forget. He stood there on stage singing a sea shanty, holding a broom handle with a light dangling from the end of it and as he was performing the piece he was swaying the light and as far as I was concerned he was really on a ship, so powerful was the performance. It was in a way similar to all the things I love about a Beckett play, minimal set nothing superfluous everything there for a reason, in a way over the years it has been a reference for a lot of my recording and painting.

35.

CATHAL O'REILLY
(THE SHADE, LUGGAGE)
KID CREOLE AND THE COCONUTS
DUBLIN, 1981

As a drummer in The Shade there were many good gigs and it was a good time to be in a band. I was sixteen when I joined so even going into a venue was a thrilling event let alone playing there. Although the places to play were not as specialised as they are now, I remember them as a sort of 'Green Acres' of show business. But they were places to play and you were certainly on the right track if you got to play in them.

I've been asked what your best gig to play was. The one that stands out in my mind was the Sportsman's Inn in Dublin. On the night we got a good crowd who enjoyed themselves. What I remember was that everything was good. What I mean is all the rehearsing (we did a lot, we needed to) paid off. Everything fell into place, the audience got it and I felt like a pro. When you and all your band mates bounce off, complement each other's playing it's a great moment, it's what you strive for.

And the best gig I ever went to? A gig that was so impressive at the time was Kid Creole and The Coconuts in the Stadium in the early '80s. I was at an Echo and the Bunnymen gig the week before, which was good, but sort of represented the mood of the time…..dark. But when Kid Creole hit the stage it was like the circus had come to town. There was so much happening on stage all at once, Coati Mundi jumping around and providing explosive percussion and the sexy Coconuts doing backing vocals and brilliant dance routines. Combined with the biggest band I had seen to date, it was powerful. There were many themes running through the show which provided a theatrical edge. I had never seen a performance like this. And the entire band smiled. It's hard to describe but being dour was the fashion at the time, so it was great to see a big band celebrate good times. I'll never forget it.

36.

DEKLAN DACHAU
(PARANOID VISIONS)
THEATRE OF HATE
DUBLIN, 1981

My Favourite Gig ever was Theatre Of Hate In McGonagles 1981. I remember it like yesterday. The fear, the expectation, the tension and the power on stage at this gig was unreal, and the poor support band Amuse who became Blue In Heaven got savaged on stage, by the angry, ugly and violent crowd! It left its mark profoundly on me! Theatre Of Hate entered this cauldron of blind hate and triumphed brilliantly with a stunning show of tribal energy I've only ever witnessed since at Killing Joke concerts.

37.

CION O'CALLAGHAN
(FREELANCE DRUMMER – PADDY CASEY, SHANE MCGOWAN)
ROCKY DE VALERA
DUBLIN, 1982

I have been going to gigs for years. There have been some awesome ones, Ben Harper in my old stomping ground The Shepherd's Bush Empire in 1998, Richie Havens in Handel's Bar on Fishamble Street (he was somehow persuaded to turn up there for a post-show drink), The Pixies in The National Stadium in 1989, Brian Wilson The Point Depot, Pearl Jam in the same venue in 2006 (even more thrilling was I played in the opening act and I met a big hero of mine in drummer Matt Cameron). The first one I remember though was when I was seven. I think my Dad was working at the Brighter Homes Exhibition in the RDS, so my Mum took me in one Friday evening. When we arrived, we met another school buddy of mine, a chap called Brian Davey. Brian's Mum knew my Mum and Brian was one of the class clowns, so we naturally got on, so the Mums decided to let Brian and myself wander off alone while they did the serious business of checking out the various exhibits.

At the back of the venue, there was a stage set up and a band, Rocky De Valera and The Gravediggers, were about to play. A small crowd gathered and Brian and I, thinking nothing other than we wanted to see what was going on clearly, moved to the front of the small crowd. Off the gig went. About half way through the gig, the drummer started having problems with one of the toms on his kit, it kept slipping off its mount and eventually fell off! Rocky (or Fredia McAnna as he was also known) was a bit taken by Brian and I, given that we were, by far, the smallest and youngest members of the small audience and we'd been standing there with smiles splitting our faces for the last thirty minutes or so! He picked up the now loose tom tom, took a couple of sticks from the drummers stick bag and called Brian and I up to the stage. For the next couple of tunes, the band let two mad young fellas bang the be jaysus out of that tom tom and during the last number, the drummer even did an extra long *'Las Vegas'* ending so we could go nuts! It was, to put it mildly, fukin' awesome! My first ever time on a stage playing drums and it wasn't the last! The drummer gave us the sticks as a souvenir and I kept it for years, only loosing it during a house move a few years ago.

I've lost count of how many gigs I've done since, thousands at least, but that one evening sticks out for obvious reasons. I never met Ferdia again and other than thanking him that evening, I never got the chance to thank him since.

38.

COLM O'DWYER
(TCD ENTS OFFICER 1991-1992)
U2
DUBLIN, 1982

Although it's very difficult to pick just one, I think that the best gig I was ever at was U2 in the Saint Francis Xavier (SFX) Hall in Dublin on 22 December 1982.

At that time, U2 were at the very early stages of the *'War'* album tour. The 3 Dublin 'pre-tour' gigs were meant to take place in a relatively small venue called the TV Club but were switched to the larger venue at the last minute due to demand. There was already a real buzz developing around the new album.

I was only 14 years old and on crutches, having broken my ankle a few weeks previously. I went with my buddy Tom Pollard who helped me to get around. We thought we would have had to stand at the back because of my crutches but U2's sound engineer, who was an absolute gent, spotted me and invited us up to join him up on the sound control desk so that we could see and hear everything.

What a gig! U2 opened with *'Out of Control'* from the *'Boy'* album and the crowd went berserk. It stayed that way for 19 or 20 songs including the new ones *'Two Hearts Beat As One'*, *'New Years Day'* and *'Sunday Bloody Sunday'*, which Bono first introduced with the famous "*this is not a rebel song*" line.

I remember it getting so hot in the hall with all of the jumping around that condensation was pouring down from the ceiling. The band were really tight and Bono, with the full mullet and cut off t-shirt, was like a dynamo, running around, climbing onto the amps, pulling girls out of the crowd, waving a giant flag. By the end of the three encores, including the mighty *'Trash, Tramoline'* and the *'Party Girl'* (another first) and *'I Will Follow'* to close, it was obvious, even to a 14 year old at one of his first gigs, that U2 were really something special. By the end of the following year they were superstars.

You can watch what was effectively the same gig as *'Live at Red Rocks'* (recorded in part as *'Under a Blood Red Sky'*), which was only seven months later.

39.

PETER JONES
(PARANOID VISIONS)
POISON GIRLS
DUBLIN, 1983

My favourite gig was back in about 1983 when I went to see Poison Girls in the Lourdes Hall in Dublin. It was particularly important to me as it was a turning point in terms of assessing what way I believed the way music should be presented. It reinforced my belief in D.I.Y. music and the way the band mingled with the audience, especially because they had just sold 50,000 albums.

40.

DARAGH MCCARTHY
(MUSICIAN, DJ, FILMMAKER: THE STARS ARE UNDERGROUND)
VIRGIN PRUNES
DUBLIN, 1983

In Northside Dublin of the early 80s when music was still tribal and important, there was a sense that your tribe chose you and not the reverse. My tribe was those slack jawed long hairs that followed barefoot convent girls around St Anne's park on Saturday afternoons before The Grove disco on Sybil Hill Road. The barefoot ones it seemed were almost always from Maryfield, just off, tree lined Griffith Avenue and it was through their older brothers' record collections that first I got my musical education. Lizzy, Gallagher, Led Zeppelin, Hawkwind and so forth.

Weekday evening efforts to avoid Irish homework entailed an hour or so listening to Pat James on the pirate Radio Dublin. He played demos by DC Nein, a band called The Frames, The Mod-Ls and singles by U2, The Atrix, Tony Koklin and new wave internationals. I remember occasionally he played tracks by Virgin Prunes who I knew were connected to U2 through something mysterious and fascinating called Lipton Village. When tracks by The Prunes came on I invariably headed to the kitchen to put the kettle on mostly avoiding the mind-scraping, painful noise they made. They were too punk for me.

They had a sound which made me, by no accident, deeply uncomfortable; until in a moment of epiphany I realised that those strange scary fuckers from Glasnevin were all just rabid Bolan and Bowie and fans. The music *all* made a sudden sense. I was sold. And I bought into the mystery. Full tilt.

They were now the coolest and most interesting band on the planet. And sat perfectly with The Velvets, Patti Smith Group, Peter Gabriel and Lou Reed records in the corner. Even though they were part of the same strange Lipton Village gang and The Edge and Dik Prune were brothers there was a real sense of the bands being the antithesis of each other with a palpable sense of light and dark, good vs evil, Beatles vs Stones. I later heard that at some point a section of the more committed U2 fans verbally attacked Gavin Friday accusing him in a serious way of playing the devil's music while U2 played God's.

They were boys that wore dresses and carried pig heads about the place in sacks - mythically. They couldn't have come out of Ireland but could only have emerged from Dublin

When I finally got to see them in 1983 at the SFX, a theatre owned by the Jesuits, it was at the end of a tour promoting ...'If I Die, I Die' their first official album on Rough Trade. I had the feeling I might have missed all the legendary performances... The support on the night if there was one might have been a Japanese duo called Frank Chickens.

There was a tall standard lamp onstage and Dik on guitar sitting down in a wooden chair all long hair like Cousin Itt. Guggi wore totter-heels, a pencil skirt. He had bleach-blond, big-hair and was smoking cigarettes like a streetwalker. Gavin came on like a Brechtian fishwife, 10 hole Doc Martens appearing occasionally from under his heavy velvet ankle length dress. He was a real physically intimidating cross dresser, a light heavyweight in a maxi dress. They all had long hair as far as I can recall which weirdly emphasized their punk rock credentials even more it seemed to me.

This was the coolest smartest thing I had ever seen. The previous year I had been bored on the hill in Slane by The Rolling Stones.

I think they opened with 'Theme For Thought' with its ponderous baseline. They certainly didn't hit the stage with an upbeat number for the kids. It felt like maybe *we* were under scrutiny and had to impress them. Brilliant.

The one song I clearly remember was 'Ballad Of The Man' by Dave-id Busaras who ambled on stage half way through the night and said in a drawn out voice half innocent "There are good people here. There are bad people here". This struck me as the most confrontational thing I'd ever seen or heard of at a concert when I thought about it.

Then the lyrics *"...came in from the underworld last night. Looking for a bank to rob, bank. He said do you wanna join my gang? I said you must be joking..."*

And I clearly remember the point where Gavin Friday, loomed over the bird-like frame of Guggi, possibly during 'Baby Turns Blue' and throttled him with a scarf like a lover. "It was an accident. I didn't meeeean it".

It wasn't by any measure the best gig I have seen but when the next day over the teatime table The *Evening Herald* was brandished at me with shock headline and photos "Transvestites simulate strangulation on stage", I figured I'd done my bit for teenage rebellion, or at least annoying the folks.

41.

WILL WALSH
(THE PLEASURE CELL, THE JOHN WAYNE MEMORIAL DANCING LIZARDMEN)
THE SMITHS
DUBLIN, 1983

I am always wary of music articles that start with the preface of "best ever" or "my favourite...." etc. So when I was approached to write this about my favourite gig/concert I was obviously dubious. However, as its all for a good cause, it was a pleasure to try and remember what might be a contender amongst a long list of very memorable gigs that I have had the pleasure to attend.

I decided rather than try to single one concert out as "my favourite," that I would like to write about one of those nights in my musical journey that I have been very lucky to be a part of. I am talking about those rare and wonderful occasions when you are made to believe that you are witnessing what may go down in the musical history books as a time when something changed. I have had a few of these moments, but the first one was probably a winter's night in December 1983 in Trinity College, Dublin when The Smiths played on their first ever tour.

I was lucky enough to gain entrance to the gig as there was a massive crowd outside the venue where a small riot broke out. This was at a time in Dublin when some of the best gigs around were at student venues and when Ents Officers had a budget and a remit to bring up and coming acts, such as Morrisey and co. to our shores. The Smiths at this point had not even released their eponymous debut album. I was aware of The Smiths due to their *'Hand in Glove'* single but I had no idea that they were or would become as legendary as they did. To think now that this was their first ever gig outside of the U.K. is quite hard to comprehend, especially when you think of how small the music scene and gigs were in Dublin at the time.

The Blades did a great support slot and then on came The Smiths to unrestrained applause and general mayhem. Flowers were strewn everywhere and Morrisey launched into what became his signature swagger, but was at the time totally fresh and radical and enthralled me and made me a huge fan to this day. If I'm honest it is difficult to remember actual songs from that night but the point is that it happened and I was there. Looking at the internet it seems that this gig never occurred. Some sites list a gig on this date at the SFX, others state that The Smiths first Dublin gig was in 1984. I was also surprised to find no reference to the riot outside the venue in which a window was broken and crowds of unhappy Smiths fans remained to catch any soundbites they could from the ferocious performance inside.

Anyway, gig over with a smile on my face, I proceeded to take the long walk home to Bray, Co.Wicklow (no taxis in 1983) and managed to get as far as UCD where I slept on a park bench, the sounds of *'This Charming Man'* still ringing in my ears.

So *'What Difference Does it Make ?'* (sic.) Well for me, apart from The John Wayne Memorial Dancing Lizardmen at The TV Club, I now realise that I have witnessed one of those moments in the chronicles of rock and roll history that changed things. The Smiths definitely made things and life in general feel different and for that I am grateful.

42.

ROY WALLACE
(TOXIC WASTE, DOCUMENTARY MAKER)
TOXIC WASTE
BREMEN, 1984

It was our first ever tour of Northern Europe as Toxic Waste. We spent several days in Amsterdam between gigs where we were introduced to local customs by the Amsterdam punks. Before we left for Bremen we all emptied and cleaned the bus.

Arriving at the German border (which was closed at that time) we were stopped and strip searched. The border Gestapo took me outside with several guards and Alsatian dogs to search the bus. They opened the back door of the bus we had been living in for the last two weeks and chucked in the dogs. Who jumped back out again.

They did this several times then let it go as I was pissing myself laughing at the situation, then they searched the bus. After everyone was suitably hassled they let us go and we got back into the bus. As we drove off waving to the guards, I noticed sitting right at the front on the windscreen was a tobacco pouch with several grammes of grass from 'The Dam' which they had somehow missed. We skinned up and headed for Bremen. When we arrived 'worse for wear' at the Slachtenhauf in Bremen we met Schaslik who insisted we drink a bottle of tequila then I passed out on the stage due to fatigue.

I woke up later with Phil kicking me as the audience had arrived while I slept. I downed a beer and started singing with Patsy. After about three songs, the audience left en mass – everyone. We thought fuck we must be particularly bad tonight! Turns out they were defending the venue from attack by Nazi skinheads and my final memory of this gig was standing outside watching Grub speeding about, Marty, Patsy & Phil tripping as a Bremen city firework display was in full swing illuminating the punks and skinheads fighting each other on waste ground while listening to 'The Cure' sound-check in the upstairs part of the venue, as they were also playing that night. The crowd eventually came back to the venue and made us play twice!

It was a great gig/party and we made lots of friends – up the Bremen Punks!

43.

PAT CLAFFERTY
(MEXICAN PETS)
THE CLASH
SFX, DUBLIN, 1984

My favourite gig. A difficult decision! I could have picked the Sonic Youth Nirvana Top Hat gig, or R.E.M in 1985 just after their Reckoning album. Or I could plump for any of the Hope gigs in the '90's. Virgin Prunes in Paris, New Order's first tour or The Smiths in the SFX, Jawbox in New York. Almost stumped. If, I had got to see The Sex Pistols, it would have been that.

So, my favourite gig was The Clash in the SFX, Dublin. Not just because the much missed venue was my second home, but the atmosphere on arriving outside was electric. Punks, skins, long-hairs, kids, dads, black and white. All gathered. I met my friend Eric and we wandered in to the darkened hall to the sounds of Dub Reggae. Even the smell seemed to reek of dope and wiser men than I.

Getting towards the stage was a slow march. Excuse me, sorry, excuse me, oops sorry...etc. We settled for behind what looked like was going to be the mosh pit. There was a deep red curtain completely across the stage. After what seemed like half an hour, the lights went down. We could see what looked like TVs or screens light up behind the curtain. The crowd began to heave and lurch a bit. The noise built. Then an English gentleman's voice over the P.A...

"Punk rockers, reggae rockers, rockabillies, ska dancers, pop Pickers, ladies and gentlemen, please welcome on stage...THE CLASH" The curtain lifted. The light behind was blinding.

Then it started...The chop guitar of *London Calling*. The band were standing on the drum kit. Indeed, those lights were hundreds of TVs. They were showing coverage from the recent Brixton and Liverpool riots. They were blinding at first. The crowd moved in a wave, forward, then got pushed back, and on it went. They performed all their greatest....Clampdown, Garageland, White Riot, and many more. But my favourite was *White Man in Hammersmith Palais*. To see Paul Simonon, bass slung impossibly low with his cool stare and wide legged, suddenly to jerk away...it was the coolest thing I'd ever seen.

But then, trouble. A bunch of idiots wearing helmets with spikes in them had injured Eric. He disappeared from view. I knew it was going to be pointless to try move around to find him. He was going to be fine, I thought. Staying behind the mosh pit, having to push the nutters back in as they got pushed out was getting tiresome. I moved back. The sound was great. The rest of the gig was great. It came to an end as people drifted slowly towards the exit among cans and fag butts and toffee wrappers. Except I couldn't see Eric. There were about 5 brave souls looking to get past the bouncer backstage. Pleading. Then I thought about Eric. Was he ok? After being sure he wasn't around, I went up to the bouncer at the backstage door. "Excuse me, I've lost my friend, I think he was injured earlier. Do you know is he inside?" Yes he is. You wanna go in? Great thanks. What? I've just been let in backstage. I climbed the metal stairs and heard noise from a room. The door was ajar and I went in. There were about 15 people in the room. I looked around and there was Eric sitting on the couch. Paul Simonon had his arm around him and they were laughing. Paul Simonon!

I had just come back from working in a print factory in Munich and had bought this very crap tan leather jacket. It was a really awful one with an elasticated waist. Then Strummer turned around and was facing me...

"Hi Joe."

"Alright mate." he said. He had the best biker jacket ever.

"Wanna trade jackets?"

"Nah mate."

Then he showed me the inside. He'd stuck on a flyer from their first tour.

"I'd never trade this."

And then he handed me a bottle of beer and left.

"See ya".

And that was it.

The Clash doctor had stitched Eric up and we left.

I remember nothing more, other than the tape bootleg was on O'Connell Bridge the next day.

And it was raining.

44.

KIERAN GLENNON
(DOCTOR NIGHTDUB – IRELAND'S PREMIER REGGAE DJ)
THE JOHN WAYNE MEMORIAL LIZARDMEN
DUBLIN, 1985

OK, this all happened in the summer of 1985. The date is worth noting, as *'The Commitments'* wasn't published until 1988. Some of this may be a bit hazy, but I think I could stare a libel lawyer in the eye and smile.

A friend of mine called Michael Murphy had been in a band called Cuba Dares, who moved to London as all bands did in those days, but he left them and moved back to Dublin. When they returned to play in Dublin, he was invited to put together a support act. And thus were born the John Wayne Memorial Dancing Lizardmen.

The John Wayne part was a minor tribute to the M.D.C. song *'John Wayne Was A Nazi'*. The Memorial part was left over from the fleeting moment when we were almost called the John Wayne Memorial Ceili Band. The Lizardmen part was a reference to the Dungeons and Dragons figures available from the iconic Dublin shop, The Diceman. The Dancing part was simply a mission statement.

The manager of a ticket agency off Grafton St had a regular night in the TV Club, a 1200-capacity venue on Harcourt St, and he printed flyers and handled ticket sales; the band he managed, a dour electronic two-piece called Ambition In Glass, were also be added to the bill.

Our modus operandi was strictly "twenty two singers, one microphone". First up was Mick Mohican, so named because he sported a Joe Strummer, Combat Rock-era mohawk. So taken was he with all things Clash, and so uncanny was the likeness, that he actually got away with travelling around the world with a photo of Joe Strummer stuck where his own passport mugshot should've been. Not surprisingly, he sang *'Know Your Rights'*.

Our second song was The Undertones *'Teenage Kicks'* performed by yours truly. I suspect I was picked to do it more so because my northern accent lent it a certain authenticity, rather than for any obvious vocal ability.

Our final vocalist was Michael ex-Cuba Dares, with a song by The Scars, the name of which escapes me, but it was basically a spoken-word rendition of the British Ministry of Defence nuclear air-raid advice, set to music. You know the kind of thing, take shelter under the kitchen table, and just think of fallout as another form of dandruff, only more toxic.

The instruments were played by guys who actually knew what they were doing: Neil on lead guitar and Barry on rhythm. Willard on drums and Mark on bass were our rhythm section.

The final item in our set list was an untitled dub-jazz-industrial instrumental workout featuring a somewhat less than orthodox rhythm section. We had decided to stay true to our Einsteurzende Neubaten sensibilities by going round town nicking the inside sections from the litter bins that used to be attached to bus stops. When thumped hard enough, these all-metal DIY bongos made a most satisfying racket. The industrial rhythm section also provided gainful employment for otherwise unoccupied vocalists.

We practiced hard for, oh, about a week and got our set down.

During the sound check, our already bloated numbers were swollen by three late additions. Bill Graham RIP had arrived to review the gig for *Hot Press*. He got so into the spirit of things that he offered to play a spare snare drum that we had. We decided to take up his kind offer as it ought to at least guarantee us a favourable review. Bill was accompanied by Fiona from *Hot Press* who played rhythm guitar.

The final recruit was a transvestite, whose name I remember as Des, and who wanted to do backing vocals. Despite the fact that none of our songs actually featured any backing vocals, we agreed to let him / her join the band on the basis that he / she claimed to have snorted coke with Keith Richards and that struck us as pretty rock n roll.

Twenty minutes before going on stage, the lads decided that our dub-jazz-instrumental thingy really could do with lyrics after all, so I was sent into the dressing room to get composing. On the back of a flyer, I scribbled together some lyrics, and *'Fear Is The Key'* was born. There was simply no time to get a melody together, so we decided to go with it as a second spoken-word piece. The transvestite was thrilled, as suddenly we did have a use for backing vocals. Unfortunately for him / her, and luckily for me, the soundman had refused point-blank to let us sound check this number, so all the vocals were conveniently lost in the mix.

Our Svengali victory was to play the film *'The Great Rock N Roll Swindle'* in the bar upstairs. This was cunningly timed to finish a few minutes before we played so the hall filled first with bodies, and then with manic laughter as we ripped through our set. I won't say it was all note-perfect but all the songs were recognisable. But by the time we finished the dub-jazz-industrial workout, the ashen-faced soundman, by now out of his head on valium, decided that enough was enough, pulled the plug and turned up the house lights. We grinned and offered to help him load the truck.

Bill Graham's glowing review duly appeared in the next issue of *Hot Press*. I think he glossed over the fact that he'd been on stage himself, but he did say that Malcolm McLaren would've been chuffed and that our punky attitude proved that laughter blew away the blues.

My one regret, looking back on it all? If only we'd thought of having a brass section, we could've had a great Spartacus moment, all going "I'm Roddy Doyle! No, I'm Roddy Doyle! NO, I'M RODDY DOYLE!"

45.

HUGO FITZGERALD
(KILL DEVIL HILL)
THE MEMBRANES, THE PLEASURE CELL, KILL DEVIL HILL
THE COMMUNIST PARTY OF IRELAND
DUBLIN, 1985

This was one of the strangest places to play a gig.

It was the first night of the *'Travelling Trash Review'* Tour.

Some remember it as a great night of music, but some remembered it more for the fact that we were paid not in money but in free Guinness, so The Membranes produced two big empty petrol cans from their van and filled them up. They were happy campers for the rest of the weekend.

46.

COLM WALSH
(MANAGER, INTOXICATING RHYTHM SECTION, SULTANS OF PING),
THE GOLDEN HORDE, THE GOREHOUNDS, THE BONESHAKERS, PARANOID VISIONS
DUBLIN, 1985.

There was a moment in Dublin in the mid 80's, when Temple Bar counter culture wasn't about shop counters. It was about a Dublin of possibilities, a Dublin of polar opposites. There was the little old lady on O'Connell Street with pictures of aborted babies alongside the fledging (it appeared) gay scene. It was the Dublin of the SPUC movement and the Militant Tenancy. There was the church's book shop Veritas countered by the Communist party's Connolly Books, there the IRA bomb factories and the Fianna Fail bugging scandals. Aidan Walsh had invented band practice and Eamon McCann was giving speeches, Richard Branson was handing out condoms and the Hare Krishnas was serving dinner. Thus, Dublin emerged with an electrifying soundtrack; Dublin Psychobily.

There were a lot of abandoned buildings, stretching from Temple Bar to Mary Street, which on a Saturday afternoon would come alive with impromptu concerts, demonstrations and markets.

With the ethics of punk rock and the ingenuity of street kids, any empty building could be a venue, squat or shop. 4 different bands could sum up for a generation what it was all about. In one venue on Saturday afternoons, you could see The Boneshakers, The Gorehounds, Paranoid Visions and The Golden Horde. Realistically, this list could be 20 or 30 bands long.

The Boneshakers kicked off, the young, skinny, neigh wirey Dave Finnegan. He was a ball of energy. You could say the bastard son of Jerry Lee Lewis and Iggy Pop. A proud Richie Taylor, god rest him looking on. Later Dave was to leave his job in McDonalds in Grafton Street and become a Commitment.

The Gorehounds were loud, brash and brilliant. Gerry and Brian from Comet records were the core of the group that once featured the late George Byrne. Famed for their contributions to various compilation albums they strangely brought together many generations of Irish music, from the Horslips *'Guru Weirdbrain'* to the Virgin Prunes *'Princess Tinymeat'*. However on this day, it was a cover version that stole the show. The Mel Tillis classic *'Ruby, Don't Take Your Love To Town'*. This was fast and furious, this was Rockabily psychosis and the garageland disease.

Paranoid Visions have always had the onerous task of being the conscience of Irish music, a counter balance to the grandeur of U2 and the insignificance of career bands. However, Deko is an immense presence on stage, combined with PA they were brilliant live. Deko was the kind of lad your mother warned you about, when soap operas had an inner city mugging, it was always a Deko lookalike what did it. Thumping bass, heavy toms and a litany of lyrics like the Rev Ian Paisley of punk. They finished off with the classic *'I Will Wallow'*.

Last but not least, I should mention, the Golden Horde. This was the classic line-up, Des, Bernie, Peter on drums, Donal on bass and of course Simon. The Horde represented a belief that stupidity, eccentricity and intellectualism could all coexist in a pop group. Flan Obrien with a Marshall Amp. The soaring wahwah of Des OByrne and the compact history of rock and roll that was Simon's persona. So you didn't see Joey at CBGBs or the Dolls at the ICA, it didn't matter Simon was bringing them all to life here in a rundown shed at the back of The Jervis hospital. *'Crash Pad Chick'*, *'I Was A Communist'*, *'Brainiac'*, *'Vampire Bat'*, the hits kept coming.

As always, memories come with a health warning, they are the least accurate of all historic archives. However in my head I am still standing there shouting for more, more, more and believing Dublin to be the centre of the universe.

47.

PAUL PAGE
(THE WHIPPING BOY)
ECHO AND THE BUNNYMEN
DUBLIN, 1985

There are those who mock the notion that music has the power to change or even save lives but I am a believer.

I grew up in Dublin's inner city in the grim eighties, a time and place devoid of any real hope. High unemployment and a spiralling heroin problem gripped the city – for an inner city kid, the road was not exactly paved with opportunities. The bar wasn't set very high - our goals were modest. Avoid trouble, finish school, lie about your address, apply for a job. Take any dead end job you were offered or leave the country and seek a life elsewhere - college was not an option.

It was against that backdrop and a stirring interest in music that I found myself at the now defunct SFX hall on Dublin's Northside in December 1985. In what was only my second gig, I went along with my cousin Myles to see this highly touted Liverpool band called Echo and the Bunnymen. My expectations weren't particularly high; my first experience of live music had been an excruciatingly uncomfortable night surrounded by screaming teens at a Frankie Goes To Hollywood show at the RDS

For a callow seventeen year old, walking into the SFX that night was like entering another world. A strange and darkly glamorous world, so far removed from my inner city upbringing. Even now the scent of hairspray or dry ice drops me right back to that time and place; the audience was predominately if not exclusively Goths and it seemed like I had discovered this weirdly wonderful sub culture, all gathered here to worship in this one dimly lit place.

The Bunnymen took to the stage shrouded in darkness, and from the moment they exploded into life I was completely and utterly transfixed. I couldn't believe the sheer power of the songs; up until that point, music was this tame thing, always listened to in a controlled environment but that night I felt it in my chest, this physical entity; the ground beneath my feet literally moved. It was the first time I had experienced music as a wild, feral force. The Bunnymen were majestic – they were right at the height of their powers, at a point where anything was possible.

Singer Ian McCulloch exuded cool and charisma while behind him, the band conjured magic from electricity; it was the most thrilling thing I had ever witnessed. We left the venue and the world looked a little different, somehow changed in a way I couldn't as yet understand. I turned to Myles and said some day we will play on that stage, in that venue, one of those brash and youthful vows we all make that are usually rapidly forgotten.

Almost ten years later, Myles and I stood side-stage, waiting to go on with our band Whipping Boy. It was a support slot with Nick Cave and the Bad Seeds, our first time playing at the SFX; Myles reminded me of our teenage vow and we both just smiled. In the intervening years, we had formed a band, made some records, got to tour the world, visiting places two inner city kids could only have ever dreamed about.

Lives changed, maybe even saved. That Bunnymen gig had lit the fuse. The power of rock and roll and its magical ability to transform and effect change. It's all over for us now but even after all these years, I am still a believer.

48.

MICK HEANEY
(JOURNALIST, DJ)
THE CRAMPS
BOSTON, 1986

The Cramps were one of those deceptively simple bands who it was easy to take for granted until they were gone, then you realise just how special they were. (The Ramones were another group in that vein – their ear-splitting show at Dublin's TV Club in 1985 could just as easily have featured here.) So when I went to see them during the summer I spent in Boston on a J-1 student work visa, I have to admit I went as much for the support group, The Screaming Blue Messiahs, as for the headline act.

Being honest, the social aspect was also important. Thanks to an American friend I'd known since childhood, I was hanging out with a bunch of Bostonians who shared the same musical tastes – punk, indie, ska, soul, even mod – and who were introducing me to new stuff like hip-hop too. They were cooler and hipper than me – though they would never say that – so they were possibly a bit blasé about going to see the Cramps, who after all had played fairly regularly in Boston down the years.

I, on the other hand, was catching as many gigs as possible, given that Ireland generally didn't feature on American punk acts' itineraries back then. So while I may not have been the biggest fan of the Cramps, the chance of seeing such a storied cult act was an opportunity not to be missed. As it happened, it was one of those nights where everything came together to produce an unforgettable show. Arriving in the venue, I was surprised to bump into not one, not two, but three different groups of friends from Ireland, also over for the summer on work visas. The expectant atmosphere before the gig was only increased by the experience of seeing these familiar faces in unexpected surroundings. Oddly, none of my Boston pals knew anyone else at the show: looking back, I have to admit that I enjoyed being the guy who knew the people in the room for a change.

Then there was the music. The Screaming Blue Messiahs kicked off in rousing style, with singer Bill Carter delivering the band's punk-infused R&B with a sharp energy. It was a belter of a set from a band then riding the crest of a wave (which would go out soon after), but when the Cramps came on stage, there was no doubt who the top dogs were. The band exuded raw charisma while showing a keen eye for showmanship. Resplendent in a gold lamé suit, Lux Interior was part rockabilly crooner, part Iggy-esque wild man, strutting in a suggestively manner that was at once ludicrously theatrical and effortlessly transgressive. Poison Ivy was even more magnificently cool. Her expression fixed in an icy stare, her burlesque gear only adding to her intimidating presence, she prowled the stage cranking a blisteringly full sound from her Gretsch guitar. Like Lux, she projected an image that was cartoonishly alluring yet also smoulderingly confident. With Nick Knox barely breaking a sweat on the drums – despite his leather gear – the band seemed at the height of their powers.

They blasted through a set that encompassed both their early horror-fixated rockabilly classics and the fuzz-drenched rock 'n' roll of their then-current album, *'A Date With Elvis'*. (Probably because of this show, that LP remains my favourite Cramps set.) It was impossible to resist, and the crowd danced up a storm. In hindsight, the fact that there were far more women in the audience than the average punk gig probably added to the party atmosphere. It was only fitting. Lux and Ivy were aficionados of obscure garage bands and schlocky B-movies who took inspiration from their obsessions to make a brand of diabolical rock 'n' roll that was utterly their own. But they were also one of rock's great love stories, two outsiders whose chemistry was evident in their stage presence that night, as well as in the sinfully infectious party music they played. They proved that rock 'n' roll was not a boys club, a point only emphasised by the late, great Lux's penchant for high heels. Not that I thought all this on the night. I was too busy dancing, talking and, frankly, trying to look good in front of the cool indie girls around me. (To no avail, I should add.) In truth, many of these insights have only occurred to me in retrospect. But that only underlines what a memorable gig the Cramps played that night: it's a show that I continue to run through my mind. It was an evening in a foreign land when music brought me back to old friends and helped me bond with new ones. At times like that, you realise that, as the saying goes, it doesn't matter where you're from, but where you're at.

49.

GARETH MURPHY
(AUTHOR, COWBOYS AND INDIANS)
U2
LONDON, 1987

I was thirteen and it was June, 1987. My mother put me on a plane to London where I was met by my father, then on tour with U2. He took me straight to Wembley Stadium where riggers paced around, banging on scaffolding as lights and amplifiers were tested. It was the day before an important milestone in the band's ascension, you could feel the sense of triumph. U2 had previously played Wembley for a 20 minute slot at Live Aid, but now, two years later, they'd sold out two shows on their own. It was also the first time I saw a real life version of my dad's stage and roof. In the rainy summer of 1985, shortly after *Live Aid*, I'd watched him build a desk-sized model which he pitched to U2 as they recorded *'The Joshua Tree'*. With its aerodynamic roof and giant PA wings, what an impressive sight it was to see it fully built in Wembley Stadium.

Dressed in my black jeans and matching black denim jacket, all hair and teenage attitude, I explored the empty stands and imagined all the football matches since 1966. Like some tribal thunderdome, Wembley Stadium is haunted by history. Meanwhile, in the portacabins backstage, U2's young and visibly strung out crew were decidedly unfriendly. I'd met them all in Windmill Lane over the previous year of preparation, and they'd always been po-faced. But now they barely said hello. Being thirteen however, I didn't care. I had an All Areas pass and fully intended to use it.

The Edge was the first to arrive. I followed him onstage and because he knew I'd just got my first electric guitar though their supplier, he very kindly let me watch him test his gear. For hours, he went through each guitar and pedal setting, talking to Joe O'Herlihy in the mixing tower through his microphone. Considering I was learning to play every U2 song, this was like being admitted to the Wizard of Oz's control room.

"I'm just not getting the sound I want" he kept repeating to the mixing tower.

He was an absolute perfectionist, the band's workaholic. The three others arrived much later that evening. A short sound check, then left almost as quickly.

For the next two days, I watched the stadium slowly fill up from morning to night. I was on the mixing tower looking across the sea of heads, thinking that brown hair is the most common colour in England, when one guy I'd never heard of took to the stage.

"Oh shit, that's the guy I was introduced to earlier".

I'd thought he was a roadie.

It was Lou Reed, whose lyrical imagery immediately caught my attention.

Little did I know that later that formative summer, I'd begin delving into a whole new musical direction. First a Lou Reed greatest hits, then '*Transformer*', then the banana album, eventually '*Berlin*' and '*Loaded*', which became faithful companions for my roller coaster ride into cannabis, girls, exams and existential torment.

They say that the music you first went crazy about, aged about 13, is what forges your ears for life. U2 were truly electrifying at their peak and I feel lucky that I saw up-close what in the end, probably drove Bono insane. I was just behind the stage on the empty stand, looking through the scrim. The view was mind-bendingly spectacular. Wembley Stadium was in ecstasy, as if some divine power was flowing through the music, as if God was about to part the clouds above. That's how it felt for me, anyway. And for a brief moment, I saw through Bono's eyes. It's strange how history works. At that milestone, as U2 conquered Britain, I happened to be the kid watching from the shadows. There's always one.

50.

REG GORDON
(PHOTOGRAPHER, THE HOPE COLLECTIVE)
SUNDAYS IN THE LATE 80'S/EARLY 90'S
MCGONAGLES (ALWAYS MCGONAGLES), DUBLIN

When I was asked me what was my favourite gig I quickly went through my list (I have many lists): Tom Waits in the Beacon in NY in '99, Sigur Ros in Madrid in '05, Fugazi in Dublin in '90? All were incredible and moved me the way music is supposed to but I'm going to cheat and suggest a series of gigs that happened in Dublin in the late 1980's that proved that music could make a real difference.

When I was growing up in Ireland in the 80's, Sundays weren't much fun: they began with mass and ended with Glenroe. The city centre was a million miles away from the cappuccino and shopping culture that exists today. Nothing opened on Sundays. They seemed to exist purely to remind you that school or work was imminent.

So when a group of young punks came together and started to promote Sunday afternoon gigs in McGonagles on South Anne Street, in partnership with Warzone in Belfast it gave us something to do. A walk into town and £2.50 gave you somewhere to hang out from 2-7pm with an endless stream of new bands to listen too, some better than others. I'm still convinced that some were formed in the bathroom 5 minutes before they went on stage and just lasted until the last note. It is one of my regrets that I never got on stage. It really was that simple.

Very quickly though, it became more than just the music: it became a community, a place where you could learn about the world around you. The venue was filled with stalls promoting a more sustainable lifestyle, stalls informing which companies tested on animals, which companies supported the arms trade etc. It was through attending these events that I became a vegetarian, it was through these events that I became aware of the travesties that corporations and governments were inflicting on the poor and indigent of the world. It is no exaggeration to say that these gigs changed the way I looked at the world.

I have many musical memories: The Instigators, DIRT, Not Our World, FUAL from Belfast, Angus the Poet telling us how much he liked the Sun, The Thermo Nuclear Neobarbaric Space Vikings from Hades(!!), all supplying a backdrop to the quiet internal revolutions that were taking place. There was also a lot of dancing, talking and fun. No bar though, bars had to close on Sunday afternoons to appease the Catholic church, in fact that made it a better experience, more "pure" if you will.

I have other memories too, silly dancing to calm down the violent mosh pits that used to occasionally form. Trying and enjoying vegan food, buying and swapping fanzines, meeting people from different places that thought similarly and supported you. I genuinely can't recall any trouble at any of the gigs.

I am older now and a lot of the anger and courage I had when I was younger has dissipated. I am no longer a vegetarian, although I constantly try to ensure the meat I eat has come from a 'good' environment. I don't go on marches as much as I used to, BUT I still don't eat McDonalds, I still don't drink Coke and I have raised my children to be aware of the inequalities that people from different cultures still experience and to be aware that their quality of life and circumstance is but an accident of birth. So there you have it my favourite gig was Sundays in late 80's/early 90's Dublin!

51.

JIM DAVIS
(TCD ENTS OFFICER 1990-1991)
PHIL CHEVRON
DUBLIN, 1990

Dublin in the 1980's was actually a lot of fun.

Yes, it was remote, conservative, clerical, blackened by acid rain, and endlessly circling the economic drain, but for all that there was some urgency in the way people created and consumed music, in the way they danced and in the manner that some other future was proposed and spoken about. As students at the time many of us were involved in the fight over abortion rights; on one side the courts, all of the political parties, the Church and a grim collection of private conservative groups and on the other a smaller constellation of women's groups, students, activists and dissidents articulating a political imagination that was coming into full bloom for the first time since the birth of the state.

One thing we had in Dublin that the establishment lacked was the ear of young people, or some of them at least. And one way we tried to connect our peers with a new set of cultural and political values was through music and dancing, and the recruitment of bands and musicians was a big part of that strategy. I wrote to Phil Chevron, a member of the Pogues, who were at the time one of the most important bands in Britain. I had been a fan of Chevron's since his days at the front of the Dublin punk band The Radiators from Space. I'd seen them on TV as a school kid and they were great. He wrote me back a letter that was gracious and supportive and offered to play a show for us in Dublin as a benefit for court costs that were accruing as a result of a case taken against students by a Christian anti-choice organization. This was in 1990 and we arranged the show for McGonagles on South Anne Street. I met him beforehand and we chatted about what was going on, about The Radiators and about his memories of earlier shows he had played there.

Though an accomplished and seasoned performer, a singer and a veteran of The Pogues world tours, not to mention his share of McGonagles gigs, I was surprised by how nervous he was at the prospect of going onstage. This small solo show in Dublin was daunting and intimidating for him. His modesty was legendary but it was his shyness and the seriousness with which he approached his art that struck me. He was most nervous about performing well and making something really good for those fans and who had come out to see and support him. It had been quite a long time since he had played a solo show in Dublin, his hometown, and by Dublin standards he was a bigshot at the time, one of the Pogues and a legend in his own right just on the basis of his work with The Radiators. But going out there alone in front of a Dublin audience was a really big deal for him and there was something extremely elegant in the way he appreciated that audience and what it meant to to him for them to show up.

It was a wonderful show. He sang accompanying himself on acoustic guitar and ran through a series of unplugged Radiators numbers and a few Pogues songs, most poignantly *'Under Clery's Clock'* and *'Thousands Are Sailing'*, then only a couple of years old and still finding it's feet in the canon of great Irish songs. The audience wanted more which is the way he liked to leave them and afterwards, elated, he wandered off into the night.

52.

PHILIP O'CONNOR
(AUTHOR, JOURNALIST, MUSICIAN, THE BANISHED)
FUGAZI, THERAPY?
DUBLIN, 1990

On September 17 1990 I saw not just the best gig I ever saw, but the best gig I ever will see.

Back then, music in Dublin was something we did and we played and we were. It was everywhere – on tinny Walkman headphones, on pirate radio, in garages and rehearsal rooms and smoky pubs filled with scary-looking punks, drunks and skinheads. But on September 17 1990 everything we knew about music – that we could do this, and that it could be powerful and communal and beautiful – was confirmed for us when Fugazi played in McGonagles.

Some of you reading this were there – and for those that weren't, it's like the Vietnam War, in that it's very hard to describe it to anyone who didn't actually experience it.

A relatively unknown band called Therapy? came on and basically blew the back wall off of the room, armed only with a strobe light, a chainsaw guitar, a bass that rumbled like a JCB and a drum kit that sounded like all forty Grand National horses landing on the other side of Beecher's Brook, with a few fallers thrown in for good measure.

It was deafening. It was terrifying. It was electrifying.

Then, with the room already in ruins from their sonic assault, Fugazi came on and blew up the debris. Bizarrely, in a room full of straight-edge heads and straight-ahead punks, all-for-one, one-for-all, these guys were like *royalty*.

They were *mythical*, such was their influence on the music we listened to and the culture we belonged to. No-one would admit it, but these were the guys we looked up to and wanted to be.

But they didn't act as if they noticed it, and maybe that is what made it so special.

They tuned up, like we tuned up.

They screwed around a little, like we screwed around a little.

Then Ian Mackay approached the mic on the far side of the stage.

And all of a sudden they weren't like us anymore.

"We are Fugazi from Washington DC. Thank you so much for coming out."

And then, with the melancholy guitar intro of *'Blueprint'*, his guitar lit the touch-paper like a blowtorch, and they blew up the room all over again.

 This was the real thing.

The sweat dripped from the ceiling.

The crowd boiled over and back across the floor like an angry sea.

And observing from the deck of the stage, Fugazi looked out over the chaos, cajoling, caressing, playing muscular, controlled, searing tones that would echo in your head and ring in your ears for days and weeks and months afterwards, sending shivers down your spine just to think of them that would never fade with time.

I'd love to pretend that I remember it all from beginning to end, but I don't.

I look back over the set list now, and I don't remember them playing some songs – and I could swear blind they played some songs that *aren't* on the list.

But that doesn't matter.

Because for one night – one tiny fraction of one dark autumn Dublin night – we looked into the mirror of that Fugazi held up to us and we saw a fleeting glimpse of ourselves, and we thought, "we can do this too – and even if we can't, at least we will always have this."

53.

DAVE O'GRADY
(PUBLICIST, GILDED ALM)
THERAPY?
NEW INN, NCAD, UCD, FOX AND PHEASANT – DUBLIN, EARLY 90'S

The venues and the dates have faded somewhat in memory but the visceral impact and sense of awe at what three hardcore fans brought to Dublin City Centre over a period of perhaps two years will never leave me. I was doing the door of the New Inn at a show Therapy? were playing, I may not have seen it but I remember Michael selling their 7" *'Meat Abstract / Punishment Kiss'* after the show on their Multi Fuckin' National label.

I remember at the time it being out of step with the musical atmosphere in the city and I wanted to know more. I followed Therapy? everywhere after that, into campus's that wouldn't have had me during the day, into bars that had no one in them the rest of the week and eventually back to Smiley's Live at 3 where my duties were finished early due to selling out and I at last, technically got paid to see them. These three reasonably pungent Northern lads in their cut off combat shorts with a drummer who looked like a film star and bass player with a penchant for dropping his kaks. Three lads who didn't talk the talk so much as run it and through it all remained affable and accessible unlike many of their swollen headed contemporaries who were ready to rock stadia as soon as stadia came to visit their ligging hangovers.

And the singer, the singer looked like a serial killer, long hair and a vague sense of detachment, maybe he was older, we couldn't see but what he played and sung, he played and sung like a wounded animal. What Therapy? had then was power, a blistering sonic maelstrom that seemed to come from nowhere, a drummer who drummed like every gig was his last (until it was) and a guitar sound that could knock you over with weight and then pierce your brain with pure melody.

'Skyward' is the one I really remember, it chugged and then soared while *'Potato Junkie'* dared go where no one else on campus dared, ridiculing the establishment and generally not giving a fuck. Then came the mini albums and their covers, this band had no eye on commercial success, no interest in breaking out of their seething precious hardcore following, the cover of *'Babyteeth'* condemning them to only the finest record shops and of course achieving all of the former. Therapy were never quite the same band again, many times since they've created great records (and arguably been an even better band) and they've succeeded in living the dream where others woke up from the nightmare but these shows were special and seared on the brains of many who attended. Three Nordie lads who, seemingly, with no effort at all could plug in and pummel all in their sight.

54.

SMILEY BOLGER
(DJ, PROMOTER, MORANS, MCGONAGLES, THE NEW INN)
THAT PETROL EMOTION
DUBLIN, 1990

Johnny Thunders at the New Inn, maybe not my favourite gig but it was pretty memorable. It would have been close to his last gig. His health wasn't great unfortunately, he was a lovely guy but the addiction is not the person and it got the better of him.

That Petrol Emotion in the New Inn. We had a wonderful PA by default because there was nowhere else to store it and the whole building was moving to the sound of the band. It was a condemned building and you could feel the place move and the gig was packed I've been at some wonderful gigs with Thin Lizzy but that was special. There were gigs in Moran's Hotel that I remember in great detail but there was so much electricity in the air that night. They were meant for greatness like many others like the blades from that period. So many magic gigs, hundreds. It was the time of a thousand bands in Dublin but it didn't happen for too many. t is difficult to hone it down but that gig was something else.

55.

NEIL DOWLING
(PROMOTER, EVENT EASE)
THE STONE ROSES
BOOTSY COLLINS
BOLT THROWER
JOHN MARTYN

STONE ROSES
JUNE 1990, MAYSFIELD LEISURE CENTRE BELFAST

We couldn't believe The Stone Roses wanted to play in war torn sectarian Belfast in 1990 in a basketball hall of all places!. We travelled up myself, best friend Collie Andrews and his sister Justine. Together with some of the dance heads from the new sides nightclub it was quite scary walking around Belfast that afternoon, but Justine's friends were in college in Queens and brought us to Kelly Cellars Bar for pints. I then went up to Maysfield at 3pm to collect the tickets and met John Squire and Mani in the car park signing autographs - really nice guys.

The doors were unusually early for a gig at 6pm. Why we asked? Well when we went in - we found out!! Inside there were 1,000 ravers all going bananas dancing to a DJ playing on stage (something most of us have never seen up to that point at a live gig!) It was a great crowd, and it felt so right being right in the middle of something positive happening both with music in general and for Belfast.

As I had previously been working with a number of promoters/acts in Dublin, I met one of my English friends Oz who was The Stones Roses sound engineer at the time. As such I ended up working as stage crew for the band as one of their crew broke his foot falling off the stage that afternoon.

So now I was watching the gig from the main balcony beside the sound desk and could see the whole gig AND was getting paid for the privilege!!!.

The Stone Roses didn't come on until 9:45pm. They started with *'I Wanna Be Adored'*. The rest was magical! An amazing gig, Even though it lasted just over an hour with no encore. To me personally, it was life changing moment as I felt this was something I'd definitely like to do for life, even if I now had to do the band equipment / PA load out for the next 3 hours!

There was no trouble at the gig and it showed a band at the height of their powers with the world at their feet. With world dominance ahead, alas it wasn't to be, but that's a whole other story!!

BOOTSY COLLINS AND HIS RUBBER BAND (WITH BERNIE WORRELL)
MEAN FIDDLER DUBLIN 1992?

Three and a half hours of non-stop pure funk from the Master. The only artist who, in twenty seven years of working at gigs, I ever asked for an autograph - a complete gent.

BOLT THROWER
MCGONAGLES DUBLIN SEPT 1990

As Myself and my best friend Colman Andrews were working as stage crew and promoter representatives for a number of promoters in Dublin but not getting paid very well for our hard work, myself and Collie (with some great help from family and friends) decided to bring over one of the new upcoming Earache Records act's Bolt Thrower. So not knowing how the music industry works - we just rang the Earache Label and asked them would Bolt Thrower like to play in Dublin. Miraculously they said yes, so off we went to book the venue, and PA, print the tickets and start to promote the show. To cut a long story short, we had four hundred fans in McGonagles with everybody stage diving and the band and ourselves loved it. Myself and Collie even did security in the pit so the bouncers couldn't attack the fans as was the norm at those gigs then. So we were the promoters, stage crew and security for our own gig. They even stayed in Collies aunt's B&B in Drumcondra that night.

This was the start of our love affair with promoting concerts and in the next two years we promoted some of the biggest names on the death metal scene including Death, Massacre, Carcass, Morgoth, Immolation, My Dying Bride, Ggfh, and Anathema.

JOHN MARTYN
EVERY TIME

Anytime working for the late John Martyn at his many *'Midnight of the Olympia'* gigs in the 1990's. Especially when playing until 3.30am on one occasion (the Olympia stage crew were NOT happy!). Absolute amazing musician and nice guy. An awful tragedy the alcohol took him.RIP

56.

EDWINA FORKIN
(TCD ENTS OFFICER 1989-1990, FILM PRODUCER)
SONIC YOUTH, NIRVANA
DUN LAOGHAIRE, 1991

I have been asked to write about my most memorable gig back in the day, and I have to say I was blessed and honoured to be at one of the most fabled Dublin gigs of the time!! Nirvana played I think with Sonic Youth, but all I can remember was how Nirvana blew me away – the place was empty, I think Eugene Lee was there if my memory serves me right!! He was always a stable at any good gig in Dublin.

But I do recall that Nirvana played to a less than half-full venue, maybe even 150 folks tops, felt bad for them. Everyone else was in the pub, but for those of us that were lucky enough to witness Kurt Cobain and his band mates, and their raw sound – wow it was electric - it was the first time I heard them and I was hooked. I think we all knew (who were actually there) we had witnessed the best gig ever - they were going to be legends in their own right!!!

Other memorable gigs for me - Seeing The Smiths & Dead Can Dance also in SFX – along with That Petrol Emotion in the New Inn, The Pogues, oh and Fugazi at McGonagles. I could keep going…… Another awesome gig was Therapy? when they played their first ever gig in Dublin in NCAD!! Loved them too!! Therapy? ended up staying in my house in Dublin, Michael Murphy played a cruel trick and told me that were straight edge, so of course I threw them a tea party with sandwiches and Mr. Kipling cakes at 1am in my flat!!! I never lived it down, but they ate everything up!!

57.

JILL FORTYCOATS
(MEXICAN PETS)
THE EX, DOG FACED HERMANS
DUBLIN, 1991

My favourite Hope gig over the years was a tough one to choose as there were so many great ones, but I've settled on The Ex and Dog Faced Hermans at The Fox and Pheasant. I remember I was working at the Lighthouse Cinema at the time and had to leg it over for the gig after me shift - I was worried about not being able to get in but I just managed it. I remember a fair amount of people who couldn't get in were sat outside on the kerb listening. There was a great atmosphere inside, both bands were amazing and it's a gig that always stayed with me - so many years have passed but it's never dimmed in my memory.

58.

FINBAR MCLOUGHLIN
(GEARHEAD NATION)
THE EX, DOG FACED HERMANS
DUBLIN, 1991

It's almost impossible to single out one gig above all others. From the late 80s through the 90s live music was a vital part of my diet, bands local and international, playing in venue big, small, surprising and ridiculous. There have been many wonderful afternoons, evenings and nights; NoMeansNo inspiring me to play, Victims Family inspiring me to give up, Blue in Heaven in Arnotts (yes, Arnotts), six band gigs in the Grattan (Not Our World, Hey Presto, Tree Ring Psychosis, the Thermos, so many bands), Los Crudos melting the White Horse, Sledgehammer in McGonagles before the fight, running the gauntlet for Snuff in the New Inn, His Hero is Gone, John Holmes and Hard to Swallow in one night in Bradford (my ears are still ringing), the unexpected pleasure of New Order at the Electric Picnic.

I think the gig that most stays with me was The Ex in the Fox and Pheasant off Capel St. I had only heard that they were like a Dutch Crass but had not heard their music, however they were so much more. Squashed onto the tiny stage in the pub, they were four people that sound like 8. The bass player ploughing through strings, Jos like a demonic Alan Wicker shouting through a loudhailer. The guitar was a hail of noise and Katerina alternating between standard drums, kettle drums and pot lids. Through the noise the music and the ideas were sublime. The highlight was *'Stupid Competitions'* with the aforementioned pot lids. I went from unaware to devotee instantly. The played a second gig that night; I went to the second gig and bought as much of their material as the money in my pocket would allow, and then some. They're still going, still brilliant, and if you hear they're playing GO.

59.

CANICE KENEALY
(ENGINE ALLEY)
PRIMAL SCREAM
DUBLIN, 1992

When I entered the venue the atmosphere was good. It seemed like this was a party and we were all invited. People gathered in friendly circles grooving to the onstage DJs and anticipation of the main act dissolved into a celebration of what the DJs were feeding and reflecting from the crowd. Most of the audience were the same age or older than me – early to mid twenties. The hall was full but it was easy to get around and I got close to the stage. It sounded. The Primals strode out and swamped straight into Step inside This House – it was classic first song as instruction/manifesto/dare. Thrilling. They were so tuned in to where the audience was at that point - how the audience had been led to their entry point - that the song/gig was a seamless continuation of the party - the effect was mesmerizing. There was a definite feeling of being "in the moment" from all corners of the room and it was no effort to maintain it.

Innes and Young in rock guitars bookended Gillespie in black and red who channelled and transcended the piece – his feet barely touched the ground for the hour or so – exhilarating stuff. *'Don't Fight it feel It'*, *'Come Together'*, *'Higher than the sun'* and more. They encored with *'No Fun'* or was it *'Cold Turkey'* (or both? And was it Oakenfold on the sounds?)

The atmosphere remained loose and spacious throughout the gig -it was so unusual to not have to push and be shoved and to be able to dance with space around you. Up to that point I'd spent my money on *'Come Together'* and *'Higher than the Sun'* but not on the LP. I ensured however, that I had a ticket for this gig – there had been glowing reports of the show- not that it was a "show" as it would be 20 years on - it was just the 'Scream live in Jan 92 and right then that **was** the eye of the hurricane.

60.

SEAN CAMPBELL
(AUTHOR, IRISH BLOOD, ENGLISH HEART)
U2
KANSAS CITY, 1992

It's tricky trying to single out a favourite concert. I could've picked The Smiths at Carlisle Sands Centre in 1986, or C Joynes with the Dead Rat Orchestra at Cambridge Junction in 2015. But the gig I think of as the most exciting and extraordinary was U2 at Arrowhead Stadium in Kansas City in 1992. I'd seen them many times before, including at the *'Longest Day'* show at Milton Kcynes Bowl in 1985, when they shared a bill with REM, The Ramones and Billy Bragg. Not many gigs beat that. But the *'Zoo TV'* tour in 1992 was especially thrilling: the band was bolder, more inventive and much looser than they'd been at any stage since the *'Boy'* tour. (Accounts of U2's gig at Dublin's TV Club in 1980 bear out this point).

I'd seen Zoo TV already in Glasgow, and later in Chicago and Iowa when I moved to the Midwest for a year of study. I knew the Kansas City concert was my last chance of catching the tour, so I made the five-hour trip from Iowa without a ticket, arriving outside the venue on the morning of the gig. It was a sunny autumnal Sunday, and the strains of *'Strange Boat'* by The Waterboys – emanating from the stadium PA – filled the empty car park outside. Spotting an open gate at one end of the venue, I followed the band's crew inside. There, the Edge's guitar tech sound-checked his way through myriad tunes (most memorably the opening riff of *'Zoo Station'*) as I gazed at the spcctacular stage installation. After a while I was noticed and ushered outside, where the ticket office – which was now open – declared the gig was sold out. A kindly American associate of U2's entourage (a friend, I think, of Willie Williams, the band's set designer) advised that I return to the venue later on, suggesting seats might be released.

I returned at show time, and noticed a scalper waving tickets at the side of the road. I stopped, bought one at face value, and headed to the venue unsure if it was genuine, forged or (most likely) a terrible seat. Entering the vast and (now) brightly lit venue as the support band (who announced themselves as 'ice cubes from sugar land', though they were in fact Sugarcubes from Iceland) suffused the cold night with convivial sounds, I proffered my ticket to the stewards. Expecting to be shown to the bleachers, I was instead ushered forwards, and forwards again, until I was close to the stage. As I climbed onto my seat (US stadium gigs featured on-field seats – on which fans typically stood – affording higher sightlines than at equivalent European concerts), I could see it was at the lip of the band's 'B-stage', a small circular stand in the middle of the crowd on which the band performed sections of the show. I knew immediately that I'd see much of the gig within arm's reach of the band. Waving at me from nearby was the kind American whom I'd spoken to earlier in the day. I told you you'd get in, he seemed to gesture to mc. As the band took to the stage, with the distressed glissando riff that heralds *'Zoo Station'*, it was clear that the gig was going to be great. Some alignment of ambience, technology and technique made it a very special concert.

Odd details remain. Watching Bono, at close quarters, pick out the chords to Bob Marley's *'Redemption Song'* on his acoustic guitar; clocking Larry Mullen's red Doc Martens as he stood a few yards from me playing his floor toms; realizing that the (live) sound the band was making in front of me on the 'B-stage' was slightly out of synch with the (amplified) feed of that sound from the stadium PA. In such moments, the ticket felt like some kind of gift, offering a devoted (if not obsessive) fan a privileged view of their favourite band as they scaled their creative heights. Twenty years later, chatting with an industry insider at Bewley's Café in Dublin, I learned that the seat I was in was reserved for the band's close circle, and that when such seats weren't claimed, they were sold quickly to fans so as not to leave empty spaces in front of the stage. The show was, in retrospect, the peak – as well as the coda – of my U2 fandom. I moved on to other things (as, of course, did they). I never did get to meet them, though, besides a brief exchange with Bono outside REM's gig at the RDS in 1989. Now, *that* was a concert …

61.

KEVIN MARTIN
(PROMOTER, EDITOR REACTOR FANZINE)
MOBY/ORBITAL/APHEX TWIN
CHICAGO, 1993

When a 1993 event flyer declared "Warning: Do not expect a rock concert," my interest was more than piqued. The punk undertones of the then emerging American rave scene were dipping a toe into the traditional live venue environs of Philadelphia's Trocadero Theatre with a stop by N.A.S.A.'s (Nocturnal Audio Sensory Awaking) See the Light Tour featuring Moby, Orbital and Aphex Twin. Billed as the first-ever "rave tour" of North America the "non-concert" provided a study for everyone with even a passing interest in the emerging electronic music.

The American rave scene almost prided itself in not only being sonically unique but also in holding events in clandestine locations. Warehouses, cellar basements, abandoned store fronts, amusement parks and farms were the most likely locations. A traditional live music venue was not the norm.

Two of the three performers were easy choices for the tour's ambitious goal of "crossing over" to to traditional rock venue while attempting to maintain the "underground" feel that was a source of pride for promoters and fans.

Moby came to the rave scene from the punk scene. He well understood the showmanship that a rock venue headliner would seem to require. Joined on stage by a well shadowed percussionist and additional keyboard player, he came closest that night to being the rock concert performance the flyer had warned against expecting. He even played a guitar on several songs. His intense passion and limitless energy showcased the deeper emotions his songs reached for. He pulled the venue's back walls into him with pleading stretches into the crowd and he ended his set standing atop his percussion pads in Messianic pose with outstretched arms reaching for the stage sides. He was exceptional but he was also the antitheses of what the flyer had promised.

Orbital's Phil and Paul Hartnoll were the English rave scenes stars du jour. Beautiful, melodic trance tracks that rolled over and wrapped around the listener were delivered from a darkened stage. The brothers were only perceptible standing behind their racks of gear by the bouncing beams of their glasses lights. The tours visuals, designed and controlled by N.A.S.A.'s Scotto, moved the focus from the stage to the floor where the choreographed I-beams and lasers danced off the backs of attendees who'd actually turned to dance and enjoy with each other.

Richard James' best known alias Aphex Twin unquestionably provided the nights most non-rock concert performance and absolutely delivered the most punk statement. He embraced the challenges of the venue and the stereotyping of electronic music performers. He was just twiddling nobs and he was trying to remain a faceless techno bollocks. He set up his home made electronic gear behind the drum riser Moby's percussionist would later use and literally sat on the stage floor. He was absolutely invisible from anywhere but the side stage he'd snuck out from. Non-rhythmic beats and live experimental tweaks of abrasive dissonance segued into beautiful, ethereal ambiance that continually challenged the listener. It was not dance music, it was not rock music. It sounded absolutely amazing on the venue's sound system and how the roof didn't cave in is a testament to the builders. It laid a gauntlet for acceptance of electronic music in the rock mainstream. It wasn't delivered by an engaging, dancing front man. It wasn't head bobbing blissful beats. It was an orchestrated aural challenge that frightened and rewarded the flabbergasted listener who couldn't tell how the sounds were being created or where they were being delivered from but couldn't help being frozen and engaged.

62.

JOHNNY BOYLE
(LIR, PUGWASH, PICTUREHOUSE, MARIANNE FAITHFULL & THE FRAMES)
RAGE AGAINST THE MACHINE
DUBLIN, 1993 AND OTHERS

I found it extremely difficult to decide on one gig that was my favourite so I've chosen to give some honourable mentions. Some I can remember vividly and others I stumbled upon by chance.

In 1993 I saw Rage Against The Machine at the Tivoli Dublin. It was one of the loudest, most energetic gigs I had witnessed up to that point in my life. I remember both my legs had bruises on them from being crushed against the barriers at the front of the stage. I lost my shirt and hobbled onto Francis St. covered in sweat from head to toe. It was ecstatic!

Two of my favourite bands from the 90's were Janes Addiction and Living Colour.

I was on tour with Marianne Faithfull in 2002 and had a night off in Melbourne. I was eating sushi and saw in a local paper that Janes Addiction were playing up the street. The guys at the door were kind enough to let us in with our MF tour badges. I didn't realise the band had reformed and got to hear some incredible songs that I thought I would never get to hear live. It was a spontaneous night and I felt very lucky.

A similar incident occurred on holiday in San Francisco in 2001. I didn't know Living Colour had reformed and again I got to see band I loved. So many American bands would bypass Ireland when touring Europe so both of these great bands had never visited our shores. I had been in the right place at the right time.

Finally, I have to mention U2 at Slane. Bono's father had passed away that week and they had a lovely tribute for him during the set. It was honest and dignified. They played an incredible set with Bullet The Blue Sky being a particular highlight. I've seen so many gigs, drum clinics and have played a lot of festivals myself. This has given me to opportunity to see a lot of bands for free which I'm very grateful for. Live music is thriving and right now it's the only feasible way for bands to survive.

Without the support of the public it cannot survive so get out there and go to gigs. Support your local bands and see some of the great homegrown talent we have.

Rock on.

63.

BARRY MCCORMACK
(JUBILEE ALL-STARS, SOLO ARTIST)
SWERVEDRIVER
DUBLIN, THE MID-NINETIES

By the time I was in my mid-twenties, and had been in a band for a few years, gig-going had become an excuse for drunken ligging and wanton carousing (it's always the guestlist interlopers talking loudly at the bar). When I was a teenager though things were very different and every gig was a test of character that came with the distinct possibility of not getting in as I was a particularly fresh-faced young lad.

I had been thrown out of an afternoon Green Day gig in the now-legendary (and then very small) Attic venue, not once, but twice for being underage (having been asked to leave I returned to cadge busfare off my mate and was led out of the venue by the jobsworth barman. My friend left the gig with me in an act of solidarity, which I still feel guilty about to this day). The next attempt was Leatherface at the Rockgarden, which again ended in ignominy and I was turned away (a gutsier friend returned to try again and snuck in past the bouncer).

So by the time I was legally able to get in to see a show I still approached the door with trepidation. What I remember of this gig--at the same Rockgarden I'd just recently been turned away from--is relatively hazy, but the thrill of even getting in I remember well. In those days bands came on and played very loudly and briefly and between-song banter was for cabaret acts. At the time Swervedriver were considered as copyists of Dinosaur Jr, Sonic youth and My Bloody Valentine, but to me and my mates they were the soundtrack to some great summers and to see them live was special. As I got lost in the throng and the wall of noise and gazed at my shoes it was hard to imagine that just a few years later I'd be one of the hardened cynics down the back at the bar quaffing pints and saying that I preferred the earlier stuff.

64.

PHIL UDELL
(JOURNALIST, STATE.IE. MEMBER OF WORD UP COLLECTIVE)
BACK TO THE PLANET
DUBLIN, 1993

To say a night of live music is capable of changing your life is usually overstating the point somewhat but sometimes it just might be true. I could probably claim that experiencing my first gig at the age of 15 (Status Quo, if you're asking) pretty much blew my mind, or that discovering the Levellers in 1990 set me on a path that would bring me to Dublin over a decade later.

I first met Back To The Planet in May 1992 when they were supporting the Levellers. Needing somewhere to stay, they ended up coming back to our house, having a bath, making breakfast in the morning and doing the washing up. I liked them very much, even more so when I actually got to see them play a few days later in London. So began an adventure that would see me and other merry souls journey around the country to see them play.

By the following year the prospect of a trip to Dublin to see them play three gigs in two days was too good to miss so, after a little bit of bother LEAVING Wales, myself and my pal Graeme arrived in the capital, had our photo taken by a Japanese tourist and then headed to the Rock Garden in Temple Bar. One of the most important tasks on trips like this was always finding somewhere to sleep, which involved using a great deal of natural charm - or just bumping into the right people.

We certainly did that night, a group of Levellers and New Model Army fans with whom we shared many mutual friends and a few drinks over the course of the evening. When the time came, myself and Graeme took up a welcome spot on the floor in Annette and Rachel's apartment, two of our new friends that night. We were to stay in the city for another day, watching the band play a bizarre free show on the Trinity College playing fields the following lunchtime before experiencing the madness of the Ball that evening. Having watched the Prodigy in the small hours of the morning, we wearily boarded a bus, then a ferry, then a coach for the long journey back to London.

How, you wonder, did this change my life? Well the gig was ok as these things go but probably not as much fun as my wedding to Annette some seven years later - nor Graeme's to Rachel. I'm sure the four children we have between us are glad we made the trip. I know I am.

65.

EILEEN HOGAN
(AUTHOR, LECTURER)
THERAPY?
LIMERICK, 1994

I was 15 years old when I attended my first proper gig. It was Belfast band Therapy?, who were touring their new album *'Troublegum'* in 1994. My friend and I cobbled together some money for our tickets to Limerick's Theatre Royal. Because of our age, we had to sit upstairs in the balcony area, where we couldn't access the bar. No matter – I was drunk with excitement. Gazing down on the older gig-goers, moshing at the front of the stage, gave me a tantalising glimpse of my future self…

I was obsessed with Therapy? in those days. The band's early offerings appealed to my sense of teen angst and my nascent urge to rebel. I wasn't sure what I was rebelling against, really. I could reimagine it now an as-yet-unarticulated dissatisfaction with the status quo, but that would be somewhat revisionist. More likely, I was just hormonal, frustrated with the mundanity of everyday life in small town Ireland, and irritated by the constraints of my parents' protection.

After the gig, flush and sporting our new Therapy? t-shirts, we ran outside into the cold January rain to find my dad who was waiting for us in his warm car. Later, as I lay in my comfortable bed, in my safe, secure and loving home, I played *'Troublegum'* over and over, and imagined that I could understand the lyrics: *'Idiots authority, promising equality/ So where is the land of the free? Stop it you're killing me'*. The words resonate more strongly now.

66.

PETESY BURNS
(TOXIC WASTE, FUAL, THE OUTCASTS, MEMBER OF WARZONE COLLECTIVE)
VICTIMS FAMILY, GROTUS
DUBLIN, 1994

That has to be Victims Family (and Grotus) in Dublin, Barnstormers as far as I remember.

We were putting them on in Belfast the next night but wanted to see both gigs so we packed a load of people into a transit, as usual, and headed down. The bands were taking turns headlining so it was Victims Family who were on before Grotus tonight. As with so many of the gigs back then it was running late so by the time Victims Family hit the stage time was quite tight. They played accordingly!

Maybe it was the frustration of having to squeeze their set into too little a time frame or maybe they were just on fire but it was like sitting in front of a giant hairdryer on full blast. We all just kept looking each other with that 'fuck me' expression that is unique to when a band blow your socks off. The drummer was playing so furiously he broke the snare a few songs in, the other boys were just completely lit. I saw a video of the gig on Youtube a few years later but it didn't quite catch the high energy electric atmosphere of the night. We all went home feeling like we'd been through a tumble dryer at full speed, ecstatic in the knowledge that we'd be witnessing the same magic the next night.

67.

TOM POLLARD
(THE PYREX BABIES)
ROLLINS BAND
DUBLIN, 1994

The head scratch to decide brought me to many venues and many great gigs, even at the last minute it was nearly the Damned in The Top Hat Ballroom for the sheer fun of it but Henry Rollins Band in The Tivoli Theatre near Christchurch in Dublin 1994 has to be relived.

I had seen Rollins play the SFX a year or two before, he was supporting some act I cannot remember due to the fact he stole the show, *'The End Of Silence'* was on release and I had not bought the album but did the morning after, his presence was immense and finally I saw this power of man and music in the flesh for the first time.

Fast forward to 1994 and Rollins Band had released *'Weight'* and he was playing Dublin, the buzz was huge and it had to be a sell out as the venue was rammed and the Tivoli wasn't small. We had every rock act on MTV come through Dublin in the 90's. From Prong to The Jesus Lizard through Biohazard, RATM, Pantera and many other macho, bellowing, hard living hard playing earnest bands, we were lapping all the power and noise up.

Rollins Band were different, they were such accomplished musicians with lineage of serious stature, Sim Cain, Melvin Gibbs, Chris Haskett and of course Henry Rollins. We were as an audience there to join in, to sing along in agreement to all he had to deliver, we got the message. Dublin was full of copped on, strong and seasoned music lovers. The sheer power of the songs, this was a different night on so many levels. The crowd were all ready to be blown away, Rollins was intense, wound, earnest and working hard, the band were so tight.

Songs like *'Fool'* and *'Liar'* were memorable because everyone sang along, again the band just kept it coming and it just blew all other bands that year out of contention. The heat and noise all blended like the crowd did, no heavy "look at me" moshing, just a brotherhood of people gripped by Henry's clear precise delivery and the musicians' intensity, lost in their delivery. So many bands followed and it was obvious Rollins Band had an influence, vocalists becoming clear and bands tightening up and more accomplished, Amen, Clutch The Bronx (to name a few) all had that style after Rollins Band most probably played their local venues too.

The walls were wet with sweat I remember posters falling off the walls as no adhesive could combat the steam band and audience generated that night. I bet they remember that gig too, if not it's their loss.

68.

KIERAN KENNEDY
(THE BLACK VELVET BAND)
THE BLACK VELVET BAND
SWITZERLAND, 1994

We were on tour in Switzerland and when a day off loomed our bass player decided that no this won't do and arranged a show in the Reichshalle a hells angel, death metal dungeon with the requisite dogs, chains, sleeping bodies in dark dank corners, angel death stares and a Sodom and Gomorrah feel about the place.

We started to play with the help of some Ken Kesey tabs, it was heavy, we had loud guitars and bashing drums and bass.

Dogs barked, a few disinterested stares and suddenly out of the darkness a body rushes forward and pukes all over the mikestand.

Now that what I call not liking the music.

69.

MICHELLE MCCARTHY
(MARKETING MANAGER, MADISON SQUARE GARDEN)
GARTH BROOKS
DUBLIN, 1995

I have a bunch of favourites but for me the most important concerts are probably my first, and what a mixed bag - Garth Brooks at The Point when he played a week-long sold out run; Phish, at the old Boston Garden, and Bon Jovi in 1995 at the RDS.

When I went to Garth Brooks, my poor mother had to take me, and I don't think she ever fully recovered. What do you do when your daughter is climbing on top of cow-gate fencing in a room of eight thousand country music fans?! A twenty-something Martina McBride opened, and then Garth took the stage. It was like nothing I had ever seen before. The crowd sang every word, of every song. I was beaming going into school the week after with my concert program.

For many, getting to experience a Phish show on New Year's Eve at The Garden is a rite of passage – I barely knew who they were, but I was a big fan of their drummer Jon Fishman, and his dresses. Looking out the windows at the Garden at thousands of people with their peter pointer in the air looking for a ticket, I really started to wonder how I might be able to get involved in the music industry, and make sure I was always inside, with a ticket.

I bought my very first cassette tape when I was seven years old, Bon Jovi - New Jersey. Going to see Bon Jovi for the first time was a major event. Once the show started I never wanted it to end. The excitement and anticipation at seeing Jon Bon Jovi in the flesh reached boiling point when he took the stage and I almost collapsed. Admittedly, twenty years later he still has the same effect on me, old habits die hard.

70.

WAYNE P SHEEHY
(PRODUCER, OWNER OCEAN STUDIOS IRELAND AND DRUMMER WITH RON WOOD)
RON WOOD
TORONTO, 1990'S

Touring the world with Ronnie Wood is an experience I hold close to my heart, it was an incredible band he had, a mixture of the Stones team, Bernard, Bobby, Chuck, Lisa and stars such as Ian McClagan and Johnny Lee Schell, for a shy Irish guy from the country it was a big show to jump into. However it was very much typical Ronnie, a family affair by the time the rehearsals were done. Keith had sent Steve Jordan into SIR to try and screw with my head (as the Wino's were also releasing a solo album the competition was fierce from the KR side). Jordan's sortie was short lived as Charlie Watts and Andy Newmark were already at the rehearsals and treating me like a kid brother, Jordan was stuck for words a rare event!

The tour was full of fun and within 2 weeks we hit Canada. There had been a death threat on Ronnie and all of the band in Montreal (a suspected security scam, but no chances were taken) so by the time we arrived in Toronto everyone was edgy. After the sound check we had the usual personal option of hotel, restaurant or stay at the venue. Ronnie and I chose to stay in the venue backstage where we had a big screen showing old black and white detective movies that we both liked.

We were both on the couch, I was more or less asleep when Ronnie wakes me and grinning points up to the open skylight about 10 feet above us. Much to our mutual amusement a very very "large" guy was attempting to lower himself into our dressing room with a bag attached to a rope full of albums. Eventually he hit the ground alongside us. As I was a proverbial Greyhound at the time I sprang to life ready to tackle our guest now christened "Meat Loaf's fatter brother " by a hysterical (laughing) Ronnie and myself, but Wolfie our brilliant English / Irish head of security storms in. Ronnie however did what I've seen other members of the Stones do before, he immediately read the situation, calmed our new guest down, poured him a Guinness had catering deliver him a meal, signed all his albums and asked him why he didn't just buy a ticket? Our friend informed us the show was sold out for months and that he'd travelled a very long way hoping to buy a ticket.

The man saw his idols show from the side of the stage, and he's probably still dropping into dressing rooms all over Canada.

71.

PAUL McDERMOTT
(DJ, FRONTLINE PROMOTIONS, FANZINE EDITOR AND LECTURER)
CATHAL COUGHLAN
AND NINE WASSIES FROM BAINNE
CORK, 1997

After 1994's *'Lost in the Former West'* The Fatima Mansions came to an end. Cathal was prevented from recording by his record company until 2000 (*'Grand Necropolitian'* was almost sneaked out on Kitchenware Records in 1996). He hadn't played a gig in Ireland in just over three years (since The Fatima Mansions had played Dublin's Tivoli on September 23, 1994 to be exact) when he announced two Cork gigs for October 1997. A gig in Cork's Kino Cinema for October 2, 1997 was to be preceded by a pub gig in Cobh. Cathal and pianist Dawn Kenny would be backed by Giordaí UaLaoighre's Nine Wassies From Bainne with whom they had been rehearsing for a couple of days, the Rob Roy gig was essentially a live rehearsal for the following night's show.

I remember there being no more than forty squashed into the back room of the Rob Roy to witness Giordaí's latest incarnation of the Wassies: Michael Mullen formerly of Wheel and Tension played Bass and David William Murray took up singing/rock god duties, The Golden Horde's Peter Kennedy was still on drums. The Wassies were transformed, watching this new band was simply breath-taking. Kennedy and Mullen were endlessly exhilarating to watch; a fantastic powerhouse of a rhythm section. Murray was part Michael Hutchence and part Lizard King; and Giordaí was now free to concentrate on his brilliant soundscapes. It shouldn't have worked, but it did and made the following year's *'Ciddy Hall'* one of the most anticipated Irish album releases of the late 90's. It remains one of the treasured albums of this time.

Cathal and Dawn Kenny were joined by Giordai, Kennedy and Mullen for an explosive run through of some old songs. I remember *'North Atlantic Wind'*, the barrage of condemnation aimed at big pharma, being typical Coughlan – all soft and soothing one moment followed by an inferno of noise the next. Halfway through the Wassies retreated and Cathal performed some newer songs simply accompanied by Kenny. *'N.C.'* and *'Dark Parlour'* were simply astonishing; we'd wait until 2000's *'Black River Falls'* to hear them again. The highlight of the gig was probably a spine-tingling version of *'The Door-To-Door Inspector'* from *'Viva Dead Ponies'* but we also got a brilliant *'Bertie's Brochures'*. The Wassies returned for the encore and we were treated to an incendiary *'The Loyaliser'* and then the beautiful *'Behind the Moon'* finished the night.

The following night's Kino gig was good but the staid atmosphere of a seated cinema couldn't match the boiling back room of the Rob Roy. Over the years I saw some incredible gigs by The Fatima Mansions, Cathal has also played some incredible shows on his own and with others; I saw the Wassies countless times in Nancy Spains and elsewhere but the Rob Roy, Cobh gig stands out. It was just one of those nights.

Cathal would release better records than *'Black River Falls'*; people argue whether *'The Sky's Awful Blue'* from 2002 or 2010's *'Rancho Tetrahedron'* is his magnum opus. For me, I go back to *'Black River Falls'* because I can't separate that album from the first time I heard its songs in Cobh.

72.

IAN PEARCE
(SPLIT RED, LOS CABRAS, THE DANGERFIELDS, COMPLY OR DIE)
ABHINANDA
BELFAST, 1998

I think it would be hard to pick out of so many, but one of the most important gigs I ever went to was Abhinanda at Giro's in Belfast (circa Summer 1997/8?) It was my first taste of a proper DIY gig and scene, and after years of liking punk and hardcore but not meeting many other like-minded people it was an eye-opener and the start of things to come, from playing in many local bands, putting on gigs, helping cook for touring bands and giving them a place to crash after the gig. That was the gig where I realised that a positive group of people could pretty much do anything they wanted.

73.

EMM GRYNER
(SOLO ARTIST, DAVID BOWIE, THE CARDIGANS, THE CAKE SALE)
DAVID BOWIE
DUBLIN, 1999

One of my most memorable gigs was playing Spirit HQ as a member of David Bowie's band. The year was 1999, I had not yet turned 25. Accustomed to doing my own solo shows, I had quite by accident been thrust into fame-world starting off by doing the late night TV show circuit in the U.S. All of these shows were in studios - in very controlled environments, with relatively controlled crowds. Then....Bowie and band and I got on a plane to Dublin and man I'll never forget the roar that erupted from the crowd when David walked onstage to start the concert. What sounded like 100,000 people losing their minds poured out of the audience as he began his song *'Life On Mars'*. A backing vocalist in the wings was I, practically deafened and absolutely surprised by the din of excitement the crowd brought that night. After 'Life On Mars' I would take to the stage.

Only after many years of doing my own touring and living of wonderful life in Ireland, did I finally decide the mystery of that phenomenal entrance of David's at the stage at Spirit. The roar was half excitement for Bowie, and half of it was something that never occurred quite the same way in other cities on that brief tour - it was as I know now the spirited bellow of true music fans - a grateful and thrilled welcome for a man who changed the world, that only the Irish could deliver.

74.

COLM O'CALLAGHAN
(BLOGGER, BLACKPOOL SENTINEL, JOURNALIST, RADIO PRODUCER)
ELVIS COSTELLO
DUBLIN, 1999

A friend of my father's blagged me in through a side door to see Depeche Mode at The City Hall in Cork in October, 1982 but, on the drive home afterwards, all I could really remember was the aggressive support set from a shambling local band called Microdisney, who were jeered and baited throughout.

"Any requests?" enquired the singer at one point.

"Get off the fucking stage, ye're shit" came a response from the middle of the crowd.

And maybe Microdisney were shit, who knows? But they certainly left a mark of sorts and, for years thereafter, I slavishly followed their fortunes and numerous misfortunes.

 I'm still not entirely sure what makes a great live show or an impactful set but I certainly know what makes a poor one and, over the many years I've since spent beside mixing desks all over the world, I've seen far more implosions than fireworks. That which makes live music so compelling and attractive in theory – unpredictability, surprise, potential, possibilities – also make it so unreliable and often so unsatisfactory an experience in practice.

There was a time when I saw twenty bands a week, every week. This was back when I had no meaningful ties or responsibilities, had few other interests and when I wore my social stamina like a badge. No show was too small, no band too pointless, no pint too flat, no toilet too nuclear, no venue too unwelcoming. During that decade in the fog, live music was one of the few things that really mattered;- forget the quality, feel the width.

But during those years I was fortunate too to see some pretty blistering stuff and I've been floored on occasion by the sheer magic of a handful of acts who, in an absolutely subjective way and for whatever reason, spun my feet like they played with my heart. I saw a nascent Radiohead at very close quarters, also saw Nirvana support Sonic Youth twice and The Frank And Walters play a magnificent set for an invited record company in a rehearsal room in Cork. I've seen The Pixies play to a largely disinterested crowd of three hundred people in Amherst, Massachusetts while they were the most exhilarating live band anywhere and saw Suede – 'the best new band in Britain' – a week after they appeared on the front of Melody Maker before they'd released a single note.

I've seen The Divine Comedy in a series of different pig-pens in London and U2 in football stadia all over Europe. I was there when The Cranberries played The College Bar in U.C.C., when Therapy? played upstairs in The White Horse and when Pulp played The Rock Garden in Crown Alley to 60 people one Saturday. And yet I'm not sure if I'll ever see a better live show than the one I saw Elvis Costello play in Dublin's National Concert Hall in April, 1999. Backed only by Steve Nieve on piano and, for a handful of numbers, by himself on acoustic guitar, Elvis played thirty songs in two hours, scattering a typically wide-ranging set with the guts of 'Painted From Memory', a collection of sassy piano-based ballads he'd recently recorded in collaboration with Burt Bacharach.

Drawing from an exceptional and far-reaching body of work that transcends the years like it does the genres, The Beloved Entertainer made every single blow count and, from the top - a searing *'Why Can't A Man Stand Alone'* from *'All This Useless Beauty'* his intentions were clear and his aim true. At his best, Elvis is a master craftsman and an often untouchable live performer and, even two hours later, was still reluctant to wrap and go. As the house lights came on, he laid into a remarkable a capella take on *'Couldn't Call It Unexpected No. 4'* and, with all of the stage mics turned off, bounced his voice off of the walls of the NCH like a bored teenager working a bionic yo-yo.

But as always, there's another context too ;- my companion that evening in the stalls was an Elvis fan who I'd met through friends. We had a shared love of good music and sport and, sixteen years, one marriage and three daughters later, still look back on our tentative first steps from Cassidy's on Camden Street around to Earlsfort Terrace in the rain. And, although neither of us would probably care to admit it, thank Elvis for taking care of the real business.

75.

FRANCES ROE
(JAM JAR JAIL)
ROCKET FROM THE CRYPT
DUBLIN, 2001

I've seen and been at too many Irish/International gigs to pick a single, total, favourite. Depending on whichever criteria you apply, some were admirably and heroically feeble, some inspiring and magnificent. Some felt significant, but their impact later evaporated, outclassed by better acts and wilder nights maybe. A couple of years worth were great, and several claim a trophy just for the endurance &/or sheer charitable spirit of the audience. Recent shows are impossible to pick through. While a band is on-going, we're in flight together and it's no time for nostalgia.

Worthy of note and notoriety from 1980s to 2000s were:

1) Pretty much any Hope Promotions gig

2) A judicious selection of U-mack shows

3) The infamous TV Club riot with the Anti-Nowhere League (first gig)

4) The Pop & Beer festival big-lads-slappy-slap-slap moment (as witnessed from stage)

5) Pre-London My Bloody Valentine in NCAD canteen in the early 80s - which to be honest, was more memorable for the night that was in it, than the music.

For me, whether you've been lucky enough to see a great band/artist doing a great performance at the top of their game, or enjoyed the slow-burn of a dubious residency in the local dive bar, it's the personal stuff of the time – yours, the performer's, the weird sticker on the hand-drier's - that makes one gig seem more important than another, and writes it into your psychic DNA. Some socio/sensory events educate your evolution - like the smell of a ladybird book in high-babies, or watching John Hurt in '1984'.

Like seeing Babes in Toyland play out their last gasp in a small Dublin venue. They were hammering out energy & genius despite the obvious tour/trench-fatigue - humans being tested & coming up diamond, playing music that matched. But that's not the gig in mind right now. This is: I've seen artier bands, I've seen rock & roll-ier bands (maybe), I've probably seen more lovable musicians, heard more intellectually challenging lyrics, and danced harder and faster at other shows. But cool or uncool, I confess, the gig that still feeds my spirit, because it broke the back of a long streak of bad luck shit and built a still-standing structure of real delight, through the power of indomitable, harmonious, macho dick-yodelling, has to be:

ROCKET FROM THE CRYPT
TEMPLE BAR MUSIC CENTRE, DUBLIN, NOVEMBER 10TH 2001

Everybody told me they were great. You missed them? Was I not at....? etc. I'd never heard them. Didn't look them up on the internet. No TV, no radio. No loaners. But whatever. If you say so. Ticket. On the night, as usual, not much in the mood to do anything. Trapped in a nosediving long distance relationship, and a work crew dominated by pack-operating cannibals, I was flatter than an underground pancake fungus, and much less motivated. I dragged on some alien glad-rags, blanked my mind against excuses, and trudged down the road to the venue, late. Fighting complex impulses to escape, I took the side door into the show and stepped into the biggest, happiest, heaving mass of fans I'd ever seen. Whoopdifuckindoo. Perched along the lip of the stage, a preposterous wall of Testosteronii-Americanus was shunting cubic tonnes of pheromones onto the room. Bwah! Bwapbwap! A fucking horn section? I thought they were punk? The band made eye-contact everywhere, freaking the increasingly-less-inhibited Irish with their weird, unwarranted friendliness. Buried on the other end, a thousand miles away, was a curled-up, red-faced, howling, living Ralph Steadman cartoon. A sweat-dripping, grease-runnelling guitar fiend, lurching on a tight, tight axis and swagging his pendular instrument one drifting inch above the boards. Drilling a vocal channel-tunnel over the heads of the crowd. Oh crap, what is this?! It's not crap, but what IS it? Bamp. BahdaDamp. BahDahDamp. BaDahDahDeDahdaDamp. The hit I'd never heard blitzkreiged into roughly fifty dimensions. Critical faculties bolted for cover. Instinctive alarm reflexes alchemised into euphoria, bouncing off crafty flourishes of consensual anxiety. That night, that band, lifted me off my leaden feet and carved a smile into my face I'd never seen before.

It was the *'Group Sounds'* tour, I think, and since then the album has roared me into battle with everything from life-cheating blokes and D.I.Y. challenges, to death-cheating turbulence and laundry glaciers. The rest of the set-list dispatched a flurry of scouts into the band's luxuriant back-catalogue and related projects. Sometimes a solid recording can beat the shit out of a half-hearted live performance. But no matter where you're coming from, the kind of expanded satisfaction that a real live smoking-hot rock & roll experience adds to playback will never be found in a couple of hundred mp3s on a memory-stick. A great gig takes place, and makes a new space within you, where you can tap into whatever the fuck worked for you that night, whenever the conditions are ripe.

Some gigs make admirers, some make sales. Great gigs make fans. Fandom is not coolness, it's happiness.

76.

EMMET GREENE
(BANDICOOT PROMOTIONS)
BOBBY CONN
CORK, 2002

This show was part of a tour to promote the *'The Golden Age'* album which is still one of my favourite albums (and album cover). Bobby Conn and band arrived onstage in whacker fashion (the worst tracksuits you could ever imagine) and belted out an amazing funk punk soul sound. The gig was not busy (with advance tixs being really bad) so I made the venue smaller (closing balcony, cutting off parts of the room with black boxes).

I also built a catwalk to soak up space. Bobby used the catwalk to full effect but the bizarre thing with this gig was a group of people who came into the show started running from either side of the room and jumping over the catwalk while Bobby was in the middle and performing.

Jumping at the same time from different sides of catwalk. By the end of the night, loads of people invaded the catwalk go go dancing with Bobby Conn. Add this amazing performance and crowd reaction with a great onstage light show (something I'm not normally into but the lighting guy did something special) and the great songs from the touring album (with some older gems) and it's a show that never leaves my mind and one of the first I always talk about.

77.

KIERAN CUNNINGHAM
(SPORTS EDITOR, THE STAR)
CATHAL COUGHLAN
CORK, 2005

They don't call it the People's Republic for nothing.

Nine years ago, Mary McAleese, the then President of Ireland, was given the freedom of Cork city and, in her address, she referred to the sense of otherness felt by the citizens of the 'real capital'.

"When I gave Seán Ó hAilpín a distinguished graduate award at his alma mater, DCU, a few weeks ago, he told me disarmingly and seriously that he would next shake my hand in September at Croke Park," said McAleese.

"It is that 'Cork-sureness' so often mistaken by the ignorant as 'cocksureness' that is the driving spirit of the people of this city and county. It is also the very attitude, the pose which gives the rest of us not born near 'the banks' a lifelong inferiority complex. We are destined to go through life apologising for not being from Cork, and being starved spectators at the feast that is Corkness."

But there are different strands of Corkness too.

And Seán Ó Faoláin, perhaps the greatest of Cork writers, summed it up best of all when turning his attention to his countymen.

"All Corkmen, you find it out sooner or later, have a hard streak in them," he wrote.

"The gentlest are the most cruel. All are cynics. Smilers are the worst. There is steel in Cork. There is flint and the spark of fire."

Ó Faoláin could have been writing about Cathal Coughlan.

The 1980s was a toxic and depressing decade in Ireland. It was a time when we needed Coughlan's salt, Coughlan's vinegar. But he'd become the guest of another nation, writing great songs that were widely praised - and widely ignored - with Microdisney. When the 1980s mutated into the 1990s, the spark of fire in Coughlan never died. With Fatima Mansions, he came up with some of his most coruscating work. The critics loved the band, but Coughlan never got the rewards that his gifts deserved. To many, he has slipped off the radar since the Mansions broke up.

But Coughlan has produced a series of exceptional solo albums, dabbled in an opera singing career in France and made a strong claim for being the greatest of Irish songwriters. His relationship with Leeside has often been a troubled one. Coughlan was often unsparing in his assessment of Cork and the claustrophobic parochialism that he found there. So he was an eyebrow-raising choice for the programme to mark Cork's elevation to European City of Culture in 2005.

Coughlan turned his anger and his energy to Flannery's Mounted Head - a concept piece about his hometown. The song titles said it all. Ophelia Crescent is Burning, Rat Poison Rendezvous, Asunderland. The venue was the atmospheric Father Mathew Hall, a Donal Óg Cusack puck-out away from the murky Lee itself. Coughlan took on the persona of Flannery - a petrol-inhaling night manager of a call centre. Think of any other Irish artist that could come up with such a character?

Coughlan, in conjunction with the Grand Necropolitan Orchestra, held the packed hall in the palm of his hand. It was a special night. I've kept the ticket, something I've rarely done. For an encore, Coughlan's rich baritone sang another song that he'd written about his hometown - 'Payday'.

'And it's payday up on Blarney Street,
And the mystery returns,
To the bookie shops and pharmacies,
And the mystery returns.'

Ten years on, the mystery hasn't faded.

78.

ROISIN NIC GHEARAILT
(M(H)AOL)
FLAMING LIPS
ELECTRIC PICNIC 2005
DEADMAUS
DUBLIN 2009

"It's hard to choose the best gig I have ever been to and so I will decline. Instead I choose to take the coward's way out and I will describe the top two gigs I have ever been to. It would be impossible to choose between the two as in every way they take joint first place. They could not be more different and yet they both had a rather profound effect on me.

To explain why these gigs had such an effect on me I should explain first that they both marked turning points in my life. Music works as the punctuation of our day to day existence. It is the exclamation mark, the full-stop and the question mark that excites and enthrals us. Songs have the ability to immortalise events, days or even periods of our lives forever. Everybody has a song that reminds us of something or someone and it doesn't matter how much time passes when we hear it, it transports us right back. Every time I think about my joint-place gigs, the memories conjure up vivid reminders of two very different and yet important turning points in my life.

The first was a Flaming Lips gig at Electric Picnic when I was sixteen. I had never listened to their music before that day and have never listened to it since and yet I can say without a shadow of a hesitation that this was the (joint) best gig I have ever been to.

It was the very start of the school term and my dad's friend had procured some extra day tickets to Electric Picnic and so myself and my parents drove down to Stradbally to make good use of them. Even that in itself was a remarkable event, as one of 4 at that point in my life I could count how many times I had spent time completely alone with my parents on one hand. My mom ended up having to spend the whole day in the car with a sudden and violent migraine and so it ended up just being myself, my dad and his friend. We wandered into the tent more by accident than design. It had already been a surreal day and this seemed to be the perfect way to finish it.

My dad had purchased me a beer (I was still at the age where alcohol was such a novelty that I would drink anything) as a nod to the fact that I was no longer a child. My dad's friend whom I had known since birth had purchased me two or three more and I was pleasantly buzzed. When the band were about three songs in my dad insisted that I clamber on to the shoulders of one of our newly acquired friends so that I can see the stage properly. As I rested on this giants (the fellow was about six foot four or five) shoulders and watched the band play I was filled with that kind of rushing sense of joy that you get when you are very young. I was having fun with my parent in a non-domestic situation. I was very definitely no longer a child. I was coming into the more adult-like era of my teenage years and that evening under the giant inflatable balls filled with glitter confetti that the Flaming Lips launched onto the crowd with reckless abandon I think both my dad and I realised it.

The other gig that came in at joint first place was of all things a Deadmaus gig. Once again I have never been a Deadmaus fan. I had never listened to his music before I went to the gig and have not ever listened to it since. And yet I remember that night as one of the single best live shows I have ever been to.

My greatest friend and at times enemy in secondary school was a boy, who for all intents and purposes will be called Jamie. Jamie and I were joined at the hip until we started 5th year. And then, as happens with so many teenage-friendships it just started to disintegrate. We hung out in different circles and had different interests. But one thing we always shared was our proximity in birthdays. For his birthday Jamie was gifted two Deadmaus tickets by one of his friends. Two nights before the gig the friend fell through and Jamie offered me the ticket as an impromptu birthday present. It was unexpected as even at that point we were no longer really, truly friends. But I accepted all the same.

Deadmaus was over 18's and as is the wont I got in no problem. Underage girls always have an easier time sweet talking bouncers than underage boys do. Jamie however did not. He ended up having to do laps of the street looking for an opening in the impenetrable wall of security. While I was waiting for him to breech the castle I shot the breeze with the people around me. And this is what struck me the most and to this day I have never experienced it since, the sheer devotion. People had literally begged, borrowed and stolen to be there that night. It was Deadmaus's only Irish gig that year and there were fans…not fans: followers from all over the country. The night was electric with excitement. These people milling around the smoking area of the Academy were filled with gratitude at the opportunity to attend this gig. Everybody was friends because everybody had a common purpose for being there. to worship Deadmaus.

When we got inside and Deadmaus started his set I felt very, very alive. That kind of music gets under your skin and beats in your chest like your heart. I held hands with Jamie for long stretches of the gig. Both of us were swaying underneath the giant disco ball connected by our sweaty palms. Afterwards there was a slightly bittersweet sense of nostalgia. That was truly the end of our friendship. It was the last thing we ever did together him and I. And yet when I think back on that night I think of it fondly. Because even our melancholy was washed over by the joy that radiated out of the place, the fans that filled the Academy to bust were so saturated with happiness that they permeated my memories. And that is the power of music, that it can change how we frame things in our mind. Music alters how we perceive our own experiences even in our innermost thoughts.

That is why they are my joint-place best gigs. Because they changed everything.

79.

EOIN DEVEREUX
(DJ, AUTHOR, DAVID BOWIE: CRITICAL PERSPECTIVES, UNDERSTANDING THE MEDIA, ASSOCIATE PROFESSOR UNIVERSITY OF LIMERICK)
MORRISSEY
OSTIA ANTICA, 2006

With the release in April 2006 of *'Ringleader of The Tormentors'*, Morrissey's adopted city of Rome had quickly become part of the singer's imaginary. The album – arguably the highest creative point in the singer's recent career – was recorded in Rome under the watchful eye of Toni Visconti and featured Ennio Morricone's sublime orchestrations. Places (Piazza Cavour, the city of Rome itself); people (Visconti, Pasilini, Magnani); films ('Accetone', 'Porcile' or 'Pigsty'); images (the Italian flag; Morrissey pictured outside Pizzeria La Monte Carlo) as well as sounds, (street noises including the distinctive Roman police siren) all figured in Morrissey's new Romanesque soundscape. The album's songs 'Life Is A Pigsty' and 'Dear God, Please Help Me', in particular, heralded a new phase in Morrissey's maturity as a chronicler of the human condition.

Some three months later, it was tipping the high 30's when we boarded the graffitied suburban train bound for the town of Ostia located about a half an hour outside Rome. As the airless battered train hurtled along the dusty tracks, I was thinking about the prospect of seeing Morrissey play later that evening in an ancient amphitheatre built by the mouth of the Tiber. And although you can never be exactly sure as to Morrissey's thinking, I wondered if the fact that the gay film director, poet, journalist and intellectual Pier Paolo Pasilini – who prescnce loomed large in Morrissey's latest record - was found murdered on the nearby beach in November 1975 was one of his reasons for playing at this particular venue.

When the train arrived in Ostia, we walked two backpacked miles in the sweltering heat to our hotel. The small hotel was booked solid with Morrissey fans, save for two elderly Americans who asked me if there was an Elvis Convention about to take place? In reply, I acknowledged the marked similarities between the two iconic singers, but said that, quiffs aside, Morrissey was far more important than Elvis.

There was no let up in the dead heat when we eventually trudged amongst the ancient 4th Century BC ruins on the way to the gig. Sustenance was found along the way in an old fashioned grocery, which sold Pizza by the slice and ice-cold litre bottles of local beer for just two euros. Replenished, we arrived at Teatro Romano Ostia Antica just in time to hear Morrissey's support act Kristeen Young play her short set. Young scaled the high notes while she pounded her keyboard like a demented dervish version of Kate Bush. Morrissey fans were (and are) divided on the merits of Young's music. At Teatro Romano Ostia Antica it was no different and while many applauded her efforts, it was clear that the crowd were impatiently waiting for the Mozfather.

At the venue, which has played host to bands such as Pink Floyd and Sonic Youth, the local hawkers were renting out cushions at one euro a piece so that you could sit on the worn steps of the ancient terrace. However, as soon as Morrissey arrived on stage it was clear that the hawkers would have been better off staying at home. Very few people sat for the eighteen-song set, choosing instead to rush to the stage in order to try and touch the singer's outstretched hands.

With his band attired in Italian football shirts, Morrissey greeted the capacity crowd by declaring 'Mamma Roma'. Beginning with The Smiths classic *'Panic'* we were treated to a mixture of songs - three from The Smiths, one cover version – *'Human Being'* by The New York Dolls with the remaining fourteen predominantly from his new album *'Ringleader of The Tormentors'*.

With a thin security presence, there were five successful stage invasions. Morrissey, clearly in good spirits, was playful with his adoring audience. He changed the lyrics of *'The Youngest Was The Most Loved'* to include the term 'bambino'. He suggested that his support act was like actress Rita Parvone. He joked about the World Cup. He told his ecstatic fans:

"As you may know, tonight Bob Dylan is playing not very far from here. I thank you for not going. You made a very wise choice."

Morrissey and his band were in top form and on a creative high. For me, the zenith of the gig was seeing Morrissey sing *'Life Is A Pigsty.'* With a watchful Oscar Wilde as his backdrop, Morrissey performed *'Pigsty'* which confronts some of the awful realities of being human. The lights of a jet making its final approach towards Leonardo Da Vinci Airport twinkled as keyboardist Mikey Farrell played the song's coda *'Auld Lang Syne'*. The gig's encore was *'Irish Blood, English Heart'* – Morrissey's account of the sometimes fractured identity of the Irish diaspora. However, in homage to the crowd and as a sign of his love affair with Rome, Morrissey changed the lyrics to "Irish Blood, Italian Heart."

I have lost count of the number of times I have seen Morrissey play. This gig, set amongst the ruins of an ancient seaside town that had - to paraphrase Morrissey's own *'Everyday Is Like Sunday'* been closed down - was the best I have ever had the good fortune to experience.

80.

JIM ROGERS
(AUTHOR, THE DEATH AND LIFE OF THE MUSIC INDUSTRY IN THE DIGITAL AGE, LECTURER)
CHRISTY MOORE
DUBLIN, 2007

Deciding on my favourite gig is a tough question. As a teenager, the greatest, fondest and most enduring memories of concerts relate to 'firsts' – first gig; the sense of euphoria from the first experience of live loud guitar; the sense of threat and danger among the hordes twenty feet from the stage at my first stadium show; and other related firsts at early gigs quite far removed from any particular musical experience or logic.

None of these 'firsts' were ever really repeated, but however pleasing it is to enjoy the nostalgia associated with them, nothing here can actually qualify as a favourite gig. On reflection, that came at a much more mature age courtesy of Christy Moore.

December 2007 was the first time I'd seen Christy Moore play live in the flesh for just over twenty years, but that experience has compelled me go at least three times a year since. Having somehow managed to ignore him since I was a teenager at Siamsa Cois Laoi in the late 1980s, that Vicar Street show made me a born again Christy-an. Why so?

Again, it's hard to define *why* we actually like something. But I think it's because a Christy Moore gig remains a 'rare' thing, irrespective of how often you've seen him before. For a start, the sheer array of moods encompassed in the repertoire delivered over the course of the show can make Christy seem out of keeping or place with even himself at times. On the evening in question here, there was outrage, rage, comedy and contemplation all woven into the set list, which itself, as is the norm, proved somewhat prone to manipulation by the audience. In fact this is the great allure of any Christy gig – while you can safely guess half of the songs that you will hear on a given evening, you can never be quite sure of what will make up the remaining quota. That night in Vicar Street was no different with songs like '*McIlhatton*', '*Motherland*' and '*Quiet Desperation*' being elevated to the starting line-up amid such ever-presents as '*Ordinary Man*', '*Ride On*' et alia and the roof-lifting '*Joxer Goes to Stuttgart*'.

Moreover, the rare character of the experience was facilitated by the smallness of the event. The intimacy of the setting made the whole event feel highly malleable. Christy's interaction with the crowd seemed as fundamental to shaping the overall experience as the content of the set-list, in so far as one had been written up. Thus, the structure and nature of the performance is never set in stone. Even the mistakes – and there were a few – simply added to the occasion. And there was also the size of the sound – with Declan Sinnott accompanying him, the pair made two guitars and one voice sound like a band.

Overall, there is a certain sense of regret when you arrive in your mid-thirties and realise that there is something that you have been missing out on for years. On that night in Vicar Street, Christy was magnetic – far more absorbing and stimulating that any slick piece of rock or pop theatre with exploding visuals on fifty-foot diameter LED screens. Crass as it sounds, I left uplifted, thoughtful and emotional, and I've been going back for more for the past eight years.

81.

CONSTANCE KEANE
(M(H)AOL)
INCUBUS
DUBLIN, 2007

I was 14 at the time and had gotten off school a few classes early to head to the gig. This was my Junior Cert year, so I'm pretty sure my mom lied on the note in my school journal saying I had to go to the dentist. While we're here - Thanks, Mom.

The gig itself had been postponed a few months earlier due to guitarist Mike Einziger's treatment for Carpel Tunnel Syndrome. I think this added to the overwhelming sense of "I cannot believe I am actually here" that washed over the entire crowd the second the lights came on. This was the first show I ever went to by a band I was completely wrapped-up in. I couldn't believe the songs I knew from my beloved CDs could be recreated and built upon so perfectly right in front of my eyes.

When I first tried to decide what the best gig I've ever been to was, I had to call my sister. She's been to over 80% of the gigs that I have. There was absolutely no hesitation in her voice:

"Incubus, 2007"

"That's what I thought too, but my answer has been the same since 2007, since the very first proper gig I went to, and am I giving the others a fair chance here?"

I am giving them a fair chance, but it's really the feelings left over from that Incubus gig that drove me to desperately want to see more and more bands as soon as I could. That feeling still hasn't left me, 8 years later.

I've been to some incredible shows since then, but Incubus, 2007, was by far the most formative. The gig itself, but also the hour and a half long journey home, spent in complete silence and awe. Thinking about it still makes me smile."

82.

THE LATE DAVID TURPIN
(ARTIST)
LAURIE ANDERSON
DUBLIN, 2007

Choosing a favourite anything is difficult, but the concert that made the biggest difference to me at the time – and continues to make the biggest difference to me – was Laurie Anderson at the Olympia Theatre in autumn 2007.

Anderson was performing her song/poem cycle '*Homeland*' as part of the Dublin Theatre Festival. As I understand it, '*Homeland*' was a piece that evolved on tour, which accounts for why the performance I saw was substantially different to the '*Homeland*' album that Anderson released in 2010. The song '*The Birds*', particularly, felt slower, eerier, more spacious than it does on record – listening to it now, I remember how it sounded in the theatre and I wonder if it really was so different, or if the context just made it *feel* different (so much of Laurie Anderson's work is, after all, about transforming things through context).

When I saw '*Homeland*', I'd been labouring on my first album in various studios for over two years, in and out of assorted bad contracts and terrible management arrangements, all without releasing a note. Seeing Anderson clarified a lot of things for me – I realised what I could permit myself. I'd often felt ashamed of approaching music from an oblique angle. I always preferred to think things through rather than feel them out, and I'd always been told that was sterile, artificial – The Wrong Way To Do It. Yet here was a concert in which everything, right down to the concert form itself, had been meticulously thought through, and was at the same time utterly humane. Watching '*Homeland*' I wondered why we are so often told that, in music, intellect is anathema to feeling.

'*Homeland*' also opened my eyes to the joys of showmanship – and of doing showmanship one's own way. I've always endeavoured to be an entertainer as much as an artist – another thing that I'm often told is The Wrong Way To Do It. Anderson, as well as being a rigorous artist, is a consummate entertainer. Take the closing moments of '*Homeland*'. After performing the penultimate song in character as '*Fenway Bergamot*', voice pitched down into a sonorous masculine timbre, Anderson proceeded to introduce and thank her band, vocal effect still in place. Suddenly, the old showbiz routine was strange and new – and somehow all the more sincere for it.

I'll also never forget the encore. As we heard the first bars of '*Let X=X*', my friend tugged my shoulder excitedly and stage-whispered "Finally! She's playing the hits!" Getting up to leave after the encore, I noticed that Lou Reed had been sitting directly behind us. He certainly didn't *look* amused, but I like to imagine that some part of him had been.

83.

PETE MURPHY
(PUBLICIST)
TOM WAITS
DUBLIN, 2008

It had been a week like no other. The week began with the HR department of the company I was working in descending on the building to let us know whether or not our positions were 'at risk'. Thankfully mine wasn't but, sadly, I lost three colleagues including my own brother. Midweek, emotions ran many directions when my wife and I discovered we were expecting our first child. And then came Friday, oh what a Friday! Not that it topped the news that we had a child coming (it couldn't possibly), but we had tickets to see Tom Waits in a circus tent in the Phoenix Park, and in anyone's book, that's a good thing surely!

I'd wanted to see Waits for years. He's something of a legend to me, and for two and a half hours on a Friday night in August, I sat enthralled, as a master storyteller told tales of circus freaks, down and outs, twisted Disney covers, heartbreak and loneliness, which all sounds very bleak, but at no point was there any melancholy in the evening's proceedings. It was more a celebration of all things broken than anything else.

From the opener, *'Lucinda/Ain't Going Down To The Well'*, through to *'Lucky Day'*, we were treated to newer songs like *'Hoist That Rag'* and *'Make It Rain'*, Island era classics like, *'Rain Dogs'* and *'Innocent When You Dream'*, but the true jewels in the crown were the rare outings for the Asylum era tracks *'Heart of Saturday Night'*, and the peerless *'Tom Traubert's Blues'*.

I've been very lucky over the years see many of my heroes live, I could have chosen Bowie at the Factory, Jon Spencer in The Village, Iggy Pop at the Mean Fiddler, Ian Dury at the Mean Fiddler, but for some reason, all the musical planets aligned on this particular evening, and it was a magical event.

84.

DES O'BYRNE
(THE GOLDEN HORDE, N.Y.C. DJ)
GÉTATCHÈW MÈKURYA AND THE EX
NEW YORK, 2008

Each Summer, some fine people at Lincoln Centre in NYC curate a fortnight of open-air concerts and events, and it's all free! I've enjoyed all types of musical fare there, from a Theremin orchestra to a Five Royales tribute, but the night my socks got blown off, involved an octogenarian Ethio sax-player.

I had come across Gétatchèw Mèkurya on the Ethiopiques compilations but never expected to see him for reals, yet here he was, Big and Honking! His band mates for the evening were Dutch band The Ex, and I discovered afterwards they had been collaborating for the past year. Together they played, with microtones and trills tumbling out of that big Tenor sax, and embedding themselves in the fuzzy harmonic rumble of the avant-garde Dutch punks. Somehow, the revved-up Addis melodies made me insanely happy, and looking around, I saw the same look on the Black and white faces of the capacity crowd.

Everybody was dancing and grinning, as Gétatchèw dominated the centre of the stage and The Ex bopped around him like they were The Undertones. It probably lasted an hour, but seven years later I can still recall the feeling of that night. It wouldn't work on paper, but it was the perfect marriage held together by the tension of overlapping worlds and the musicality of its principals.

85.

VONA GROARKE
(AUTHOR, SPINDRIFT)
RICHARD HAWLEY
DERBYSHIRE, 2009

And not just for the name of the venue, though The Devil's Arse certainly sounds like someplace you'd want to spend an evening. December 2009. We're a group of maybe a couple of hundred bobble hats and scarves, some portion of a mile into the earth, in a cave in Derbyshire. Richard Hawley is due on any minute. He won't be trussed up, however, because it's hard to play guitar with mittens on, so we've been warned he'll perform for an hour only, before frostbite sets in and each of his digits falls off (and gets auctioned on eBay).

He comes out like a guy who's down on his luck in a Raymond Chandler plot, all double-breasted overcoat and a lot of attitude. But it's the voice that wins. It always does. Something about the acoustics here, the way what's a dark brown voice to begin with acquires an extra layer of lacquer. It's a voice for indoors, for back rooms, for pubs; a voice with smoke and mirrors in it. And it fits right into this stubborn cave, turns the place and its various darknesses inside out, to something like a seam of silver in a lump of coal.

86.

ROB FLYNN
(THE WINTER PASSING)
HAVE HEART
DUBLIN, 2009

My favourite gig of all time was July 8th, 2009 when Have Heart played a basement venue at the top of Stephens Green in Dublin, Rise and Fall played that show too actually along with local band Famine! I had just finished my leaving cert and was finally free to discover the hardcore scene in Dublin. I feel like at the age I was in the mind frame I had, that night something changed. It's like my eyes, ears and mind opened up on new levels for the very first time, it made me think!!! I think that show and every other one I attended after in a vibrant Dublin scene really shaped me all round as a human I feel. I'll never forget it. Whopper show, bought so much merch!!

87.

ROBBIE ROBINSON
(FILM DIRECTOR, AN IRISH EXORCISM AND MEMBER OF THE INTOXICATING RHYTHM SECTION, CAPTAIN TRIPPS)
KINGS X
LONDON, 2009

The greatest gig ever? That's easy. The date was 22nd of January 2009. The venue was the Electric Ballroom in London. The band was a trio from Texas called KINGS X. The reason why it was the greatest gig ever is easy too. There are musicians that can take you places They make a spiritual connection and slowly become the soundtrack of your life. Their music documents those big moments in your world. Good or bad. Everybody has a favorite band. Their songs mean something. Their music makes them feel. KINGS X were my band. They took me places. And nobody, nobody took me places like KINGS X. It's no surprise that they are called the first church of rock and roll. So on a dark and damp night in London, as those that make the pilgrimage filed into the Electric Ballroom, excitement hung in the air. We were going someplace. Over my head I could hear music.

How do you describe a group of musicians whose abilities and performance levels seem to come from another world? Bassist Dug Pinnick leads the charge, all twisting limbs and soulful grace. The bass sound is monstrous; a primordial swamp of funk n' roll. The tone moves you. Awakens you. You twist. You roll. Then there is that voice. Oh my God, that voice. It soars with the angels. Something pure. Something noble. Something good. But a voice so lived in, so wracked with emotion that it reveals truth at every turn. Dug Pinnick is not a preacher but he is a truth-teller. His, is a gift that could only be bestowed on somebody as they stood at a dusty, lonely crossroads late at night. If it's not a deal with the devil, it's certainly a loner. His voice floats over the crowd. He cuts through our secrets straight to our souls.

Beside Dug Pinnick stands Ty Tybor on guitar and vocals. He is my absolute favorite guitarist since Jimi Hendrix. Yes, he is that good. Coaching notes from his instrument that always seems to complement the song, never over-power it. But when he does fly. When Mr Tybor does decide to cut loose. His ability is otherworldly. Solo after solo effortlessly peeled off in rapid succession. It's what guitar players are supposes to do. You know when guitar players use to exist. Before it becomes all about the pedals.

On the drums in Gerry Gaskill they possess simply the greatest timekeeper operating in rock music today; the hypnotic beats are highlighted by bouts of explosive percussion. His power is breathtaking to behold. It would take a fleet of drummers to copy how he attacks the ride cymbal alone. Gerry had us dancing. We all started jumping

They kick off the set with Groove Machine, Gerry Gaskill laying down an early declaration of intent. Next is *'What is it?'* A song bullying with restrained power. *'Lost in Germany'* drops. The crowd moves as one. Swaying with the music. The songs are timeless. Black Flag, Dogman, Looking for Love. They play *'Summerland'* and we are transported away to another place. Endless green fields stretch out before us. It is the death of the season We are finally getting old. *'Goldbox'* is performed next and the band turns the vocal mikes out towards the crowd. It was that sort of night. Then they play *'Over My Head'* and the first church of rock and roll is reborn anew. Reminded why they are there. Reconnected to the world.

We fall out into the night, better from the experience.

The greatest gig of all time- You better believe it.

88.

AIDAN WALSH
(MUSICIAN, REHEARSAL ROOM PROPRIETOR)
AIDAN WALSH AND THE SCREAMING EAGLES
DUBLIN, 2010

My favourite gig/concert was the gig I did with the bucket guys in the Button Factory back in 2010... march maybe, Mundy was on bass, David Bracken on drums, David Linehan on guitar & vocals, Conor Linehan on keyboards... the Aristocrats the guys from Ashbourne Co. Meath all performed very well on the night, and all of them wore the luminous shorts with buckets over their heads...

Paddy Dunning sang a number, Eamon Carr was MC, Frank from Flip in Temple Bar got up on stage and Steve Rock, Jim Rock's younger brother performed too. The band did what i wanted, the bucket guys wore luminous shorts and the band were in their underwear and they weren't afraid to take their tops off

We performed *'Rock My Brainy Head'* and the songs off my album *'I Was On A Rocking Horse'* for most of the night, Bono or Guggi or Gavin Friday couldn't make it; on the night David and the band stole the show.

89.

DAVE LONG
(INTO PARADISE)
THERAPY?
DUBLIN, 2010

I went to see Therapy? perform their *'Troublegum'* album a few years ago in Vicar Street. 'Perform' seems to be the wrong word but I am loathe to use the phrase 'rock out'.

I'm always a little nervous when a band tours a classic album years after it has made an impression on my musical life. However, there was no need for nerves on this night.

In I went, a slightly disillusioned middle-aged man, but I emerged as a sweat-soaked, fired-up creature who I hadn't met in a while. It was a night of pure, raw energy & I wanted more.

Thank you Mr. Cairns

90.

BRIAN CROSBY
(BELL X1, THE CAKE SALE, PRODUCER)
SUFJAN STEVENS
BERLIN, 2011

So many gigs over the years, but this one stands out for the sheer joy of it.

I tend to be pretty geeky at gigs, checking out the gear, seeing what's been played live, getting distracted by any technical issues, all that super picky stuff which I find difficult to turn off. I must have bought the last ticket for this show - I was seated in the top back seat of this huge indoor theatre in Berlin, my head almost touching the roof. The sound was actually pretty amazing considering. Sufjan was only playing songs from his new record 'The Age of Adz', an electro beat driven futuristic sounding record which I had only just bought and listened to once. To be honest, I wasn't sure if I liked it so much on first listen - it was such a radical departure from his other records which I such a fan of, and which served as the soundtrack to a road trip I made across America many years previous. So perhaps my expectations were low with the knowledge that he was only playing new material on this tour. Hearing it live though and experiencing the energy of the music along with the visuals were just mind blowing. I simply got lost in the music from the first song and really didn't want the gig to finish. All said, it was a pretty slick ass production from Sufjan and the band, but it had a lot of soul. This was a wonderful, truly wonderful show.

91.

ELLIE & LOUISE MACNAMARA
(HEATHERS)
THE MOUNTAIN GOATS
BLOOMINGTON, INDIANA, 2011

We've been lucky enough to see and also play with some of our favourite artists throughout our years as Heathers. However, seeing John Darnielle of the Mountain Goats play at Plan-it-X Fest 2011 in Bloomington, Indiana definitely stands out as one of the best. We spent our teens listening to the Mountain Goats. Their music was definitely a major influence on Heathers, especially on our early songwriting. We don't often cover songs as we're terrible at remembering lyrics but one of the first songs that we did cover was *'This Year'* by the Mountain Goats.

After releasing our first album *'Here, Not There'* on the Plan-it-X label, we were invited to play at the 2011 festival. We couldn't believe that John Darnielle was also on the bill. We had previously seen him play in Whelans in Dublin but this gig was particularly special. Out of the blue, he invited us on stage to sing *'This Year'* with him. In our early awkwardness, this seemed like a nightmare at first, but ended up being one of our journey's most memorable moments.

There was something special about listening to John Darnielle play the songs that inspired us to start making music in the first place, and even more special about joining him to play one.

92.

MICHELLE DOYLE
(SISSY)
THE RAINCOATS
SEATTLE, 2012

A few years ago, I did an exchange while in art college to Vancouver in Canada. Despite being hooked up with some awesome punks over there who took me in under their wing, I was a total boring hermit. I decided to do around 28 credits in college instead of the recommended 12, so spent loads of time by myself in the 24 hours access college. It was both sad and nice to focus on art, however if I did it again I would have gone to more gigs instead of being a creepy loner.

When I discovered The Raincoats were playing in Seattle, I threw away all my work for the weekend and decided to go see them. I got into music via a Riot Grrrl Ireland proboard forum, Lastfm and Napster. I downloaded Sleater-Kinney, which opened up Bikini Kill, then The Slits, X-ray Spex and of course, The Raincoats! You'd think going to a city three hours away would be straight forward, but you have to get your E1-11 and be grilled at the border for over two hours. The officer asked me why I was going and looked up the gig on the internet. Also, he didn't find it funny when I asked if he was going too.

I got to the gig three hours early so I could ask anyone and everyone for a place to stay. I had no luck however and ended up staying in a dodgy hostel hugging my passport. The support acts, which included Grass Widow were dark and dreamy. It's sort of what you'd expect from the mise en scène of Seattle. However The Raincoats weren't just dark, they were lively; a total laugh but also incredibly dark when they needed to be. They were playing songs they wrote while in art college in their twenties, now sounded different, more layered and more knowing from performing them later in life. They were incredibly energetic and tight. I forgot just how dynamic and experimental they were. On stage they were whistling, imitating seagulls and circuit bending, while still being faithful to their songs.

They never stopped being playful. I partially went because in the last few years we've lost Ari Up and Poly Styrene, so I made an extra effort to see the bands I like in case it's the last time they ever play. It was sad before The Raincoats played *"57 Ways To End It All"*, Ana da Silva said "As the time of death approaches I want to live more. When you're young you think you're invincible". It was a perfect celebration of life and death. All that was missing was their most prolific Seattle fan, Kurt Cobain, who they dedicated the set to.

93.

JUSTIN McDAID
(FREELANCE JOURNALIST, GOLDENPLEC)
ENABLERS
DUBLIN, 2013

A lone microphone stood like a proprietary flag planted in the centre of the dancefloor. On the stage behind it, three men began to play while another encircled the mic, stalking the fringes of the ring of shadowy spectators who seemed almost too intimidated to come any closer. When 'Hands Up Who Wants To Die' kicked off proper, their reluctance proved warranted. The singer chose indiscriminately - screaming into one face, turning on his heels and giving another a hard eyeball - aware of each person's presence, but really, seeing no-one. By the time he made it up onto the stage the microphone was obsolete as he screamed lyrics from the beyond the monitors, barely audible above the noise behemoth to his rear. It was as aurally-eviscerating a set as I'd had the pleasure of seeing, and this was still only in the half hour before Enablers came onstage.

Since 2004's 'End Note' Enablers have prowled along the edges of a Venn diagram somewhere between Slint and Shellac, with the spoken-word intensity of lyricist Pete Simonelli crackling over a band that seems so tightly wound they're about to blow apart in shards of sonic disorder. Although they'd visited these lands before this appearance in The Loft was their first live show, with Simonelli goading a crowd that was still shaken from the support band's fourth wall shattering performance - "Don't be stand-offish, this is not Berlin."

From there on in it was a masterclass in the ebb and flow of suspense. Simonelli stalked the stage like a bug-eyed madman, snapping his body forward at the waist to spit a line of acerbic prose into the mic or else ignoring it altogether, orating unamplified all the while as he walked past it, unconcerned about whether it picked up his voice or not. Words tumbled out on the crescendos of drumrolls or between the gaps in the band's post-rock intricacies, unrelentingly coiling the set into a knotted device that seemed fit to explode. We could all feel it.

It was going somewhere; building to the final release of a tension that had been wrought since the first snare crack, when the set was cut short in a criminal act. The Beady Eye aftershow disco was taking place in the same room that very evening. The Beady fucking Eye aftershow disco was responsible for this most finely and intensely executed of sets being derailed before its potential was fully realised. Someone stole one of the band's guitars later that same night.

Swans are the only band I've seen since who could equal that gut-punch mastery of climatic friction. Enablers have yet to return. Maybe they never will; come back to finish what they started. Maybe that just renders this gig all the more mythical.

94.

JIM CARROLL
(BROADCASTER, JOURNALIST, THE IRISH TIMES)
THE GLOAMING
DUBLIN, 2014

I've a theory that I drag out every so often. It's about the stop sign. When you're a teen or a twentysomething, you're often all about music. You know the new bands, go to the best gigs, absorb every piece of music around. It's your badge of identity.

In your late twenties, though, something changes. Suddenly, music doesn't matter as much because there's a job, a partner, children, a house, other commitments to take up the slack. Real life intrudes. You see a blasted stop sign and music doesn't matter as much. You put the badge away.

Me, I was one of those who raced past that stop sign and kept going.

Kept heading for the horizon. Kept going for the bright lights on the edge of the next town. Kept the badge on. Kept searching for the rapture.

The rapture is what happens when you see and hear a band who make the hairs on the back of your neck stand tall. An act who send shivers up and down your spine. A musician or musicians who make you as giddy as a goat. Once you experienced it, you believe in the rapture.

You remember all those encounters too.

> Arcade Fire in a tent in Co Laois.
> The Waterboys several times when they were chasing the big music for all it was worth.
> Public Enemy bringing the noise at the Brixton Academy.
> Iggy Pop in a field in the middle of the Swiss Alps.
> Fugazi's emotional musical metrics in McGonagles.
> Johnny Cash pushing the man-in-black agenda at a matinee gig in Dublin's Olympia.
> Prince's super-sized funk in a small room in Austin, Texas.
> Van Morrison at Dublin's Stadium (when he had the fever and was fiercely and furiously following a star only he could see in the sky).
> Jay-Z and Kanye West watching the throne.

It's a long list.

Thing is, you keep chasing the rapture because you're always seeking to replicate that high. That communal buzz of being in a room when a band just fucking go for it. When they let loose. When they soar and glide and fly and freak out. When they slip their moorings and let nature take them where nature takes them.

Martin Hayes from The Gloaming gave me a great quote in the noon-time still of a Feakle pub a while back about moments like that.

"When the music is really going well, you feel like you're just participating in it. You feel like it's just happening to you, with you and out of you. You feel like you're made yourself transparent enough for the music to flow. It takes in your whole physical being, your emotional being, your spiritual being. You gradually break down the barriers of resistance to that. You eventually become physically and emotionally more free. This is what we're trying to do, have a complete flow of music and feeling over the course of a night."

The Gloaming know all about class of thing. Their show at Dublin's National Concert Hall in January 2014 was the last time I experienced that feeling of sheer euphoric mania at a live show.

Every scintilla of that show had something to treasure. Every shape and sound reminded you of just why music matters so much to deluded schmucks like me and you. It was a gig with eating and drinking galore and you gobbled it all up. Every moment mattered. Every heart was lifted. Every eye was a-glow. The rapture, live and loose on Earlsfort Terrace.

95.

COLIN COULTER
(LECTURER, AUTHOR, CO-EDITOR IRELAND UNDER AUSTERITY)
RUEFREX
BELFAST, 2014

Central to the allure of punk rock was and remains the incitement to learn a few chords and form a band. As a child in the mid 1970s, I witnessed the power of punk's DIY ethic first hand. My elder brother had an insatiable appetite for, and an encyclopedic knowledge of, popular music. And yet he had never even considered learning an instrument until '*New Rose*' ignited in his final year at school. The flowering of punk created possibilities for our Tom and his mates in the same way that it did for working class kids elsewhere. Energies that had previously been channeled into the delinquent pastimes of a very troubled north Belfast would soon find more creative outlets. It would soon become apparent that among that band of tearaways there was no shortage of untapped talent. One of them had an ear for a tune, another a gift for the telling phrase. The introspective, scrawny wee lad that had previously gone under the radar had spent his reclusive teenage years becoming a demon guitarist. The hothead from up the road managed to splice a menacing stage presence with a voice of disarming purity. After a time the four of them settled on the improbable stage name of Ruefrex.

My first experience of live music was going to see our Tom and his mates play. Ruefrex appeared at many of the venues that are now part of the hallowed lore of Northern Irish punk – the Harp bar, the Trident, the Ulster Hall. But the band often strayed well beyond the established punk rock circuit, often accepting invitations to play venues in places where few of their contemporaries would have dared to tread. On occasion, those early gigs would descend into chaos. I still remember well the evening when a local church hall was trashed after some louts from the Shankill turned up to settle some imaginary score or other. While several members of the band had reputations as lads not to be crossed, their politics were fiercely critical of the violence that surrounded them growing up. This political stance took no little personal courage. Check out the Ruefrex documentary '*Cross The Line*' and skip forward to the part where they perform the incendiary '*Adult Games*'. The footage of that particular song, a searing critique of paramilitary violence, was captured in a north Belfast community centre that at other times was known to double as the haunt of some of the city's most notorious loyalist killers. Few of their contemporaries had tunes to match Ruefrex and even fewer had their nerve.

Last year, I organized a conference devoted to the events that unfolded in October 1977 when the Clash were scheduled to play in Belfast but the gig was cancelled hours before the band were due on stage. The closing event of the weekend was a fundraiser for the organization then still known as *Strummerville* which provides gig and rehearsal space for aspiring musicians. The headline act that night was Ruefrex. While that gig was not the greatest I have ever seen – the Cocteau Twins in the Ulster Hall in November 1986 is unlikely to be surpassed - it remains my favourite. The band had only performed once in the previous two decades and had just three rehearsals prior to the night but this was a concert that will live long in the memory. The few dozen souls that turned up to support a worthy cause were offered a reminder of why one journalist – whose impeccable taste in music was alas accompanied by an utter ignorance of geography – had been moved to declare Ruefrex the 'most important band in Britain.' Looking back, it becomes ever clearer that the band really were an anomaly in the recent history of popular culture of this island – four working class lads from unionist backgrounds, with fine tunes and radical politics who had no time for conventions that punk was meant to dissolve but would instead reproduce in a heartbeat. It is little wonder then that Ruefrex have been all but airbrushed out of the official narratives of Irish popular music history.

96.

SUZANNE RHATIGAN
(SINGER, PROMOTER)
GRACE JONES
ELECTRIC PICNIC, 2015

What makes a gig great? How to pick one favourite gig to write about?

Was it Neil Young solo at the Beacon Theater NY in the early nineties because of it's utter Neil Youngness? or was it The Beastie Boys and Run DMC at the Brixton Academy mid eighties for it's ferocity and ice cold coolness? Was it John Martyn holding court in the Mean Fiddler or Prince slaying Wembley Arena? I guess if you're only as good as your last hit, I would have say my favourite gig is one of the most recent.

The indomitable Grace Jones at Electric Picnic 2015. Believe the hype, even Grace Jones couldn't over hype Grace Jones. Putting aside her back story of wild antics and eccentricities, her unpredictability etc; taking into consideration her seniority, which was irrelevant, nothing prepared me for this astonishing performance.

Much is talked about Grace Jones physical presence, and yes she is extraordinary. Her long long body atop 10cm heels, dressed in skeletal tribal paint with matching corset and thong, glistening with a satin sheen of perspiration; her never ending supply of preposterous headdresses feathers on feathers on feathers; her energy, focus, intensity, desire; her professionalism; her world class band, not to mention the HITS culminating in the truly mind blowing Slave to the Rhythm, during which Grace rotated a hula hoop around her fatless waist as she prowled the stage never dropping a note never mind the hoop, all came together to produce an hour of 'pinch me am I dreaming' entertainment!

My absolute favourite… until the next one

97.

HENRY CLUNEY
(STIFF LITTLE FINGERS, X-SLF)
SOLO
BLACKPOOL, 2015

Favourite gig was recent...just a few weeks ago...Rebellion in Blackpool, solo. I was playing the acoustic room for the second time. First time was great too...2012...however I didn't know how ill I was at the time. This time the crowd were just magnificent to me. Got standing ovations and was sure someone famous had walked on behind me! Just a magical time.

98.

JOHN O'FLYNN
(AUTHOR, THE IRISHNESS OF IRISH MUSIC)
MAPPING POPULAR MUSIC
DUBLIN, 2015

Before I get started I need to put my short contribution in perspective. As a music lecturer at St Pats College, DCU I teach a range of theory and musicology courses (including some modules on popular music), and along with Aine Mangaoang I'm currently involved in a twelve-month research project entitled 'Mapping Popular Music in Dublin' which receives its funding from Failte Ireland (mappingpopularmusicindublin.wordpress.com). What follows is a very brief 'memory mapping' of some of my own personal engagement with popular music in the city.

I would have to describe myself as one of those music academics who, while passionate about many kinds of music has largely traversed a classical performance route. That said, I've done a bit of 'free' singing, dabbling on keyboards, pop cello parts and song arranging/writing during student days and beyond, mostly in the folk/pop sphere. Looking back, it would have been amazing to have been in the midst of Dublin's post-punk scenes in the 80s but most of what I sought from live music at that time had to have a mainly acoustic line-up. Broadcasts and disco were another matter –coming from a North Dublin teenage tribe had meant keeping up with the weekly Top of the Pops and MTV Europe selections along with occasional head-banging at the legendary Grove in Raheny. Later, classical music studies abroad would largely keep me aloof from emerging club scenes… at least until I discovered Sides (and my inner dance self) in 1991. But it would be almost a decade later that I gained a whole new respect for and engagement with live rock/pop gigs, and this came about initially through research. My PhD work was based on audience responses (in terms of music and identity) across a range of classical, popular and trad events, mostly around Dublin and Limerick. Yes, there you have it, the total geek route to appreciating live popular music: do a PhD.! But as roundabout and strange as this route has been, it's one that has deeply influenced my understanding of all music, and of what really counts when approaching studies in music.

So, whizzing forward to more recent months, I've relived a lot of earlier excitement through involvement in the Mapping Popular Music in Dublin project. Some personal highlights from 'fieldwork' over the past six months (but by no means an exhaustive list) include performances by James Vincent McMorrow and We Cut Corners at the 2015 Meteor Choice Awards; the general fun of 'hearing' Dublin amidst books and vinyl during Record Store Day/Weekend in a 'songline' that stretched from Capel Street to Dawson street – and it was great to hear the likes of Mundy perform in an intimate setting, and Crayonsmith setting up Saturday evening celebrations at Panti Bar; occupying the alcohol-free oasis that was 'Paddy's Day Unlocked', where for the first time I got to see the wonderful Hare Squead, a relatively new and infectiously uplifting hip-hop/pop act from south-west Dublin.

 Now, in case you think this is all too celebratory, I can offer some balance by reporting on how awkward gig attendance has felt on rare occasions. Top of the uncomfortable list has to be arriving (too) early on a Friday afternoon at Longitude in Marlay Park last July; while I knew that I would likely be above the mean age of attendees at the festival, nothing prepared me for the gap-year-meets-Magaluf atmosphere (which was very definitely un-unlocked) that would dominate well into the evening until later arrivals helped balance things out. On reflection though, I have a measure of admiration for these current day youth tribes who mobilise themselves to attend the plethora of high quality festivals that have sprung up over the past decade and a half. The personal highlight for me was Edinburgh band Young Fathers who occupied a slot on the Heineken stage that same Friday. I had no idea what to expect but quickly became captivated by what those guys had to say, their depth of sound, their nuanced performance of race, class, sexuality and place, their compelling yet grave melodic and rhythmic lines, and their seamless integration of dance. I was transported to 'imagined-real' places far beyond board shorts, ponchos and floral wellies, but more importantly, I forget I was wearing my own researcher cap, at least for those forty minutes or so.

99.

CLODAGH SPUD
(FANZINE EDITOR)
RUDE PRIDE, THE SULTANS, TAKERS AND USERS, THE DIVILS
DUBLIN AND BELFAST, NOVEMBER 2015

In early November, I had the blues. I was stuck in a rut, pissed off with my lot and there seemed very little point...in anything really, least of all driving a Spanish oi band to their two gigs in Ireland. I considered making an excuse not to do it, spend the weekend in my jammies, isolated and feeling sorry for myself. But then, I pulled myself together and told myself not to be a flake, I had told Byrneos I would help him drive and I knew seeing some bands and an adventure like this would do me good.

You could also say this story began in March 2015 because no gig happens in a vacuum does it? I spent a weekend in Madrid visiting an old friend in her new life there. We somehow found the rock bar in the suburbs where the gig had moved at the last minute and watched Rude Pride, Lions Law, Saints and Sinners play to an adoring afternoon crowd. Contacts were made and a two day tour of Ireland was planned as a result of some Irish punks and skins being at this show.

So where was I? Sharing food my partner and I made in a Dublin punk house with the band from Madrid who would play that night. I really like the tunes they play: super-catchy street punk with lyrics in English that address racism, sexism, fascism and celebrate skinhead culture. I come from a DIY punk background and all this "oi" is new to me. I really hoped the lads would be cool.

One of them enquired if we knew the Irish band Easpa Measa. Yeah we do! The two of us were in that band. Turns out this guy put on our gig in Madrid in November 2007. No way! We're all grinning and remarking on how small this punk community is.

So on to the gig: The Divils, Takers and Users played solid sets, the The Sultans - a good time posi oi band formed in Dublin by three immigrant punks. Their album "wobbly oi" is my sound track for beer drinking sessions and road trips. I know every word and sang along smiling. The boys brought an enthusiastic crew from Hungary. When Rude Pride play they looked at home with the borrowed equipment, they play a blinder but there are a few broken strings to stall things a little bit. In their set the band cover Blitz *'New Age'* and play *'Career Opportunities'* by The Clash.

Next day, my partner Byrneos and I drive the band in two cars to Belfast. As per the rules of tour, an English speaker who is willing to chat can ride "shot gun" (so that the driver doesn't get bored or drowsy). Miguel sits up front and we have the craic trading local history lessons, tour stories and opinions on the differences between skinheads in different countries. He tells me that he shat out the window of a moving car on tour once, so naturally I became nervous any time he rolled down the window from that point on. I was really interested to hear about the scene in Madrid. When I was there in March, a fella on his own began throwing shapes at the motley Irish crew I was loitering with, it transpired he thought we were dogy right wing skins (I'm not sure how anyone could jump to that conclusion about me or my hippy mate Sarah). "He was going to fight us all!" I said to Miguel. That's Madrid apparently, nazi skins will not be tolerated. The aforementioned incident ended with us all going for a beer together. On a practical note, some of the Madrid SHARP skins are helping Syrian refugees to find accommodation in the city.

Upon arrival in Belfast I get lost (as usual) but eventually find the venue and a place to park. After some excellent curry, we knuckle down to the most important part of touring with a band: waiting around. There was a really nice friendly atmosphere in the venue and I met some mates from different parts of the country and some new heads. Tonight, Takers and Users kick off proceedings with tight as fuck street punk, Aggressors BC mellow things a bit with their sweet dual vocal attack of political reggae, The Sultans provide tunes to dance to/sing along with and Rude Pride once more pull it out of the bag. Belfast loves 'em.

I was really tired and would love to have guzzled a few pints however, my driving duties are more important and I spend my cash on recent releases by Aggressors BC and 1000 Drunken Nights instead. Much later at the apartment where I will sleep for a couple of hours, a wonderful couple chat to us about Belfast in the bad old days. They were in their 50s and although I wanted to hear their stories, I could barely keep my eyes open. They insisted we take their bed and we gratefully lay down for a bit of shut eye.

After dropping the half-locked Madrilenos to the airport (now just a bunch of bad smelling scruffy looking skins) I began my 2.5 hour journey home. Alone in the car, I started to process the weekend I'd just had and felt very positive. I really have so much to be grateful for: Sharing laughs, brilliant music, the generosity that defines punk rock community, old/new friends across the generations and good politics. This will be my favourite gig...until the next one!

100.

PAUL PURCELL
(DJ, FOUNDER OF GLACIAL SOUNDS RECORD LABEL)
SWING TING
MANCHESTER, 2015

My favourite experience of a live show took place in Manchester in October 2015. The party I played was the monthly Swing Ting at Soup Kitchen in the Northern Quarter of the city. I had previously worked with the Swing Ting guys on some projects as they also function as a production team and label. Expectations were high, for both the party and the venue, as I had been consistently hearing amazing reports. Needless to say it didn't disappoint. Swing Ting has cultivated something special in terms of the regular attendees, so the crowd was really receptive to the variety of stuff I play. The set was also hosted by the crews MC, Fox, who really controlled the crowd and added to my enjoyment of playing. The venue was great, 250/300 capacity basement with amazing sound. I spent the majority of the time I wasn't playing on the dance floor and avoided the green room trap (I didn't realise there was one until the end) which is testament to how much fun it was really.

101.

MICHAEL MCCAUGHAN
(TCD ENTS OFFICER 1984-1985, AUTHOR, THE PRICE OF OUR SOULS: GAS, SHELL AND IRELAND)
JELLO BIAFRA AND THE GUANTANAMO SCHOOL OF MEDICINE
DUBLIN, 2015

"AREYOUFOURTEEN?" yells a kid in a baseball cap and studded punk jacket.

What, Me?

I am leaping about up the front as Jello practises his double act of singer and mime artist. Since when did he turn into Marcel Marceau? It is very funny. Could it be to quell the disappointment that he's not getting his usual four hour rant and release time? Yes, sometimes even Jello doesn't know when to shut up. And neither do I. Tonight Mr Biafra is on a righteous rampage, his Guantanamo School of Medicine grinding out hard core punk rhythms and surf guitar rip currents in glorious gut-crushing intensity, a reminder that the DKs not only whipped everyone else's ass at the time but also made it onto the pop charts.

"What?" I ask.

I visited the US in 1987, hoping to catch the Dead Kennedys only to discover they had just split up. Don't mention the war.

"AREYOUFOURTEEN"?

Christ, who is this guy and what does he want.

There is a brief respite between songs.

"What?" I ask.

The punk cadet finally becomes audible-

"ARE YOU FLIRTING?"

Thirty years ago one of us would have ended up in Accident and Emergency for the likes of that.

Tonight however, we merely giggle.

I've spent the past twenty five years in Latin America where the daily equivalent of the front stage mosh pit is performed daily on the metro and buses of Bogota, Mexico City and Buenos Aires. Try squeezing your way onto the Transmilenio in Bogota at rush hour and you will be lifted off your feet, swept along and possibly remain airborne until you arrive at your destination. Minus whatever you had in your pockets. Now that what I call hardcore.

It's been a while since I've been up the front at a punk outing and I realise there's been some changes. The first major gig I attended was the Specials and Dr Feelgood in Dublin, 1979, a teenager bunking off school on the pretext of attending a charismatic catholic revival event. As Jello himself once observed, the greater the lie, the easier believed. Back then there was an air of menace and imminent violence which might just decide to pick you out of the crowd. Hence the relevance of 'Nazi Punks Fuck Off'. I was terrified. A couple of skinheads climbed up on the speaker stack that night, dragging them down as mayhem erupted. Soon after, at another 'catholic revival event', in Maynooth University, I watched as the Virgin Prunes were 'escorted' off the stage amidst scenes of chaos and fighting by homophobic punks/skins known as, I kid you not, the Black Catholics. Absurdly, Maynooth University was the seat of training for the priesthood, so you could call it serendipity. Then there was the Magnet, a sketchy venue in the centre of town where the Outcasts played a series of electrifying gigs. I loved the muscular riffs and the rockabilly energy but hid behind a pillar when the lead singer took off his studded belt and began whacking someone who said something to him. I always associated Punk with that hint of menace - *'GIVEUSTENPENCE'.*

Now however, the scene has changed. The young punk disappears, smiling all the time, the mood is cheerful, supportive and relaxed. Jello takes a stage dive and I'm thinking wow, it's been a while, gripped by a sudden urge to do likewise. My first stage dive was at a Teardrop Explodes gig in 1981, marking the beginning of a career which lasted till the mid 1990s, coinciding with the untimely death of my Mohawk. When my mother first saw the Mohawk, she gasped. 'You had such beautiful hair', she said, before the ominous sentence, 'you'll be bald at thirty'. She was right, almost to the day. Long live the mothers of this world.

Stage diving turned distinctly uncool over the years as drunken yobs hurled themselves carelessly at the crowd, fists and boots flying without a thought. There's an art to the stage dive but few took the time to study it. Idly, I think to myself, if he plays *Holiday in Cambodia*, I'm heading for the stage. But it's not going to happen. I'd heard Jello no longer played any DK numbers.

Jello prefaces each track with brief, pithy, political messages which hit home. He explains the three strikes rule before asking whether Michael O'Leary has started building prisons-for-profit in Ireland. He talks about austerity, refugees and racism, burning issues of the day and it feels like a charismatic CSPE teacher has occupied the stage, delivering bite size nuggets of wisdom. Greed and corruption are the key watchwords, he says, pointing the finger at THEM, while refugees and racism are staring in our direction and demand a response. "Make rich people pay their taxes", he says, launching in to 'Barrack-star Obama,' deconstructing and dismissing another US President.

Near the end of the gig Jello strips off his shirt and gets help from a roadie to put his bra on. He is still flapping and miming and engaging in all sorts of tomfoolery, a perpetual plastic smile glued on, mimicking the targets of his ire. He seems to be channelling some inner ageing former US President wandering about the corridors of his mansion in his pyjamas.

I'm not familiar enough with the Guantanamo School of Medicine albums to distinguish tracks but the sound is tight, the drumming superb and I make a mental note to stock up on the albums. There follows a lecture on Iran and Afghanistan and the manner in which the US builds its insurgent forces (Taliban) and allies (Saddam) only to launch wars against them when their interests no longer coincide.

Biafra sprinkles some of the classics into the mix, the 'Government Flu' and 'California Uber Alles' before o no, say it ain't so, I hear the opening bars of that song. It summons up every act of injustice perpetrated throughout Latin America, every assassinated activist, every stifled hope, every *Campesino* who raised a machete in defiance, every mother searching for her disappeared child.

There's no stopping now as I am possessed by this strange inner connection between a bass line and a people's history, a drum roll and an insurrection and the lyrics that made rebellion not simply possible but urgent and overdue.

I eye up the stage. Jello has flown, now it's my turn. I edge myself up and stand tall, signalling my intent before self-launching into the tightly-massed front rows. I disappear downwards as gravity triumphs and my head rapidly approaches the floor. What possessed me, I wonder, briefly, before I am lifted upwards by a small army of angelic teenage punks. Gently, I float, it is utterly peaceful up here. As I steady myself back to my feet a skinhead approaches and places my cap back on my head.

I decided it was long past bedtime and headed for home, a cup of tea and a slice of toast ahead. Punk died in 1977 but is born anew, the baton handed on through the years as the scene evolves. When it comes to wit and wordplay Jello has few peers. How about the 'The Audacity of Hype' for an album title (Google it, you'll see why) and on and on. Jello is angry, indignant and wise, his band a potent cocktail of punk nobility. Long may they reign.

102.

GARRY O'NEILL
(CULTURAL HISTORIAN, AUTHOR, WHERE WERE YOU?)
VARIOUS

In the late 1970s/early 1980s only two things mattered, music and football. Live music came second to buying, listening, swapping or stealing records, but living close to venues like the National Stadium on the S.C. Rd, TV Club on Harcourt Street, Olympic Ballroom on Pleasant Street and McGonagles on South Anne Street meant it was never too far away. Older brothers often subsidised fees in the case of the old local Dandelion Market gig, with bigger gigs it was a case of assisting you in trying to get in and that only happened if it didn't hamper themselves or their mates' attempts to gain entry, as often happened at Trinity College, Mansion House and McGonagles gigs, leaving one to stroll home wondering what might have been.

There was certainly no chance of tagging along if a gig was out of town, thus ruling out The Grand in Cabra, Stardust in Artane and Belfield UCD. I vividly recall waiting up to hear the stories, an animated telling of the Dexys Midnight Runners gig in the Mansion House along with a souvenir programme from the gig kept me enthralled for weeks. Tales of stabbings, Gardaí beatings, fights with rival gangs, great new bands and craic all combined to make to the gig world overtly exciting.

I recall hanging around outside venues in order to catch a sound check in the hope of blagging a guest list/ticket, it worked sometimes as with The Pogues in the SFX. Come gig time if you hadn't gotten in it meant listening outside while conspiring to bunk in. Waiting for someone inside the gig to open a side door/fire exit of the venue was another method of entry, I recall the Olympic Ballroom being good for that for a while. My mates and I would habitually arrive at a gig and try bunk in regardless of who was playing, with the Stadium being the preferred venue by the mid-80s. We caught lots of half decent gigs there by Moving Hearts, Leonard Cohen, Depeche Mode, Elvis Costello and Everything But The Girl.

Outside the Stadium a ticket stub procured from a punter leaving early, and there was quite a few of over the years, was enough to get in. Two old brothers who worked the front gate knew me from attending the amateur boxing nights and always let me in with said stub as you needed it to get pass security at the top of the stairs inside the main entry doors. Other times they'd open the doors as a band neared the end of their set, propelling you to hurriedly dodge past emerging patrons who were off to get the last bus or a comfy post-gig drinking spot at a local bar, enabling you to catch a couple of songs and/or an encore or two. There were dozens of gigs but this is a snap shot of just some of them.

The Specials gig at the Olympic Ballroom as part of the 2-Tone tour in Nov '79 was one the first gigs, myself and school mates from James Street gained entry via a side door. Bunking into The Stranglers gig at the Stadium on *The Raven* tour was another early highlight. There were early OMD and UB40 gigs also at the Stadium around '81/82, the UB40 one marred by some bad fighting outside beforehand, and Dexys Midnight Runners at the same venue the time of their *Too-Rye-Ay* album, a gig which seemed quite intense. Good craic was had losing my jacket at SLF in the TV Club in '82 and losing a shoe up the front at a more dance orientated sounding New Order gig in the SFX in '83.

There was a great series of reggae gigs in the TV Club between '83/84 with British groups like Aswad, Steel Pulse and Misty in Roots alongside Jamaican acts such as Dillinger, Sugar Minott, Tapper Zukie and Clint Eastwood & General Saint, all observed and absorbed with cheap hash and even cheaper wine.

Other reggae gigs worth a mention included LKJ/Dennis Bovell & the Dub Band in the SFX in 83, Toots & the Maytals in Hawkins around '86, Sly & Robbie's Taxi Connection tour featuring Yellowman/Half Pint/Ini Kamoze at the Stadium in '86 and Black Uhuru also at the Stadium. Desmond Dekker & Laurel Aiken in Smiley Bolger's wonderfully small New Inn venue on New Street around '90 plus later gigs by the Mighty Diamonds at the Olympia, Brigadier Jerry at Firehouse Skank and The Congos/Culture both in the Village and Junior Murvin in Crawdaddy.

Another LKJ gig in the Gaiety, a reading of his poetry with no accompanying music which some punters failed to notice on the gig posters, ended up with me separating two groups I knew but who didn't know each other. Behind sat a bunch of local lads from Chamber Street disgruntled with the omission of a band but loudly laughing along to the words to LKJ's *Lorraine*, while in front sat a few out of town Trinity students calling towards the lads for quiet/hush only to be met with aggressive threats of violence which thankfully didn't materialise, probably due to the copious amounts of hash being consumed rather than my pacifying skills.

There were lots of gigs in the mid-80s. The Fall with Ms Brix Smith in the TV Club in '84, a slightly surreal gig as it came a couple of days after serving a four week stretch in the old Meath Hospital. The first gigs by The Smiths in the SFX also in '84. I dug Johnny Marr's hair and guitar. The Ramones two gigs at a jam-packed TV Club in June '85, touring the *Too Tough To Die* album. Those gigs were probably responsible for the longest sustained period of post-gig ringing in my ears. I spent the second night on the balcony overlooking the stage with a bunch of Northern Irish punks in Dickies and Devo adorned leather jackets.

A Pogues/Golden Horde gig in McGonagles around '85 was divided between dancing and staring at their young bassist Cait O'Riordan. Good gigs by British psychobilly band The Stingrays/Golden Horde plus The Milkshakes/Those Handsome Devils both in the TV Club. Mick Jones' Big Audio Dynamite in the SFX with Schooly D and other rap acts as support around '86. I liked the debut album and was looking forward to the gig, especially after seeing the Strummer/Simonon/Hired hands incarnation of The Clash limp over the line at the SFX a year or so previously. A good gig spoiled somewhat by a few punk saps spitting and calling for Clash songs and Joe Strummer. There was a good Aztec Camera gig in McGonagles and a couple of exceptional free lunchtime gigs in Trinity College of which The Blades and The Go-Betweens stand out.

There were some good blues gigs in the late 80s. BB King and Buddy Guy in the Stadium come to mind, also a great series of gigs upstairs in the old Weford Inn which later became the Village. If memory serves me correct they always seemed to take place on a wet mid-week evening with the Mary Stokes Band as support. They featured blues singer from the southern states of the USA, amongst them Carey Bell from Mississippi, Louisiana Red from Alabama and Lazy Lester from Louisiana.

Late 80s/early 90s gigs I remember were Public Enemy in McGonagles in May '88, Fugazi/Not Our World also in McGonagles around the same time. 100 Men, a Doncaster skinhead band who played authentic sounding rocksteady, No Means No and Ruff Ruff & Ready gigs all in the New Inn around '90/'91. Radical Dance Faction in the Rock Garden plus The LA's in McGonagles and Iggy Pop gig in the Stadium around '88/89.

Drugs enhanced some gigs throughout those years. I recall taking speed called 'pink champagne' before both Slayer's gig in the Top Hat Ballroom in Dun Laoghaire and Megadeth's gig in the Olympic Ballroom. Taking micro dot/double dipped strawberry acid before Happy Mondays/Shaman gig in McGonagles, The Orb in the Point, Gary Clail & On-U Soundsystem in Sides? and Jah Wobble's Invaders of the Heart in the Rock Garden. While nearly everybody apart from the not very undercover Gardaí seemed to be on ecstasy at the Primal Scream/Andy Weatherall gig in the SFX in 1992.

There were good nights at Midnight at the Olympia, gigs by Stereolab/Tortoise and a lively Ian Dury and the Blockheads amongst the more memorable. A sold out gig by The Beastie Boys/Scary Eire in the Tivoli in June '94 was another great night, one of my fondest as it nearly didn't happen when my guest list didn't look like materializing as Gardaí arrived to usher away the ticketless crowd outside. A whistle turned my head to see a mate in the Tivoli entrance waving a ticket in my direct. A hundred yard backtrack, two understanding Garda and one haggling doorman later and that was that.

Other gigs included Bo Diddley in the Mean Fiddler. US3 and a great Bootsy Collins gig in the Tivoli, Terry Callier in Vicar Street, Jimmy Smith in the RDS Library, plus a great pair of gigs by Nick Cave & Bad Seeds/Dirty Three in the Gaiety and Fela Kuti's old drummer Tony Allen in the City Arts Centre. There was also a Bowie gig at the Factory in Barrow Street, a secret invite only affair for an anniversary gig for the Quadrophonic drum & bass club night; he played a set of his current drum & bass material followed by a set of hits.

I recall trying to talk about bootlegs to a pretty gruff Dave Thomas at the bar after an excellent Pere Ubu gig in the Mean Fiddler around '98. Zen Guerrilla supporting Man or Astroman in the Music Centre. There was Acid Mothers Temple in Whelans, The Beta Band, Plaid and Autechre gigs in the Music Centre. Japanese band Corneilius supporting Flaming Lips in Olympia and a Can solo projects gig also at the Olympia, both around '99. Motorhead in Vicar Street in May '01, the last night before the venue had to adjust their noise level capacity owing to previous local residents' complaints, what an appropriate band for that occasion. Planxty's reunion gig in Vicar Street in '04 was special, as was Kraftwerk in the Olympia the same year, the most crystal clear sounding gig ever.

More recent gigs by Wilco Johnson with Norman Watt-Roy in the Leeson Lounge, PIL in Tripod/Button Factory and Jurassic 5 in Vicar Street were all pretty good also. A few London gigs over the years would be up there too, such as Half Man Half Biscuit in Dingwalls, Burning Spear in the Town & Country Club, plus a Bad Brains gig at the Astoria.

But I think the most memorable of all the gigs I was at were ones by bands/singers that I liked but never thought I'd ever get to see. They included three gigs in the Stadium around 86/87, a hot and smokey John Lee Hooker gig, a wonderful Ray Charles show, and a rip roaring night by American soul diva Millie Jackson doing her sexed up funk thang. The other two gigs were two quite mesmerizing performances in the Gaiety by The Blue Nile in Sep '90 and the wonderfully aching sweet voice of Jimmy Scott in Mar '01.

103.

TERRY O'NEILL
(MANAGER OF THIN LIZZY AND OTHERS, AS WELL AS A PROMOTER AND PUBLICIST)
VARIOUS

I saw Tom Waits in The Olympia Dublin, The Band in The Royal Albert Hall, Brian Wilson in The Royal Festival Hall, Joni Mitchell in The RDS, Van Morrison many times in Dublin, Waterford, Clare and London, Bob Dylan many times in Dublin, Meath, London and New York. They were all absolutely brilliant shows....can't say more than that except....amazing, wonderful, incredible, inspirational, unforgettable etc. etc

104.

ANTO DILLON
(EDITOR, LOSERDOM FANZINE)
VARIOUS

I'm sure most people who are replying to this question have the same initial response - it's a very hard question to answer, to pinpoint one gig as my favourite out of all the amazing gigs I've seen in my lifetime, almost all of which are special for some reason or other. To be honest I can't pick out one gig in particular so I'm going to write about some that stick out in my mind for various reasons.

JACKBEAST
(AT THE BAMBI RELEASE GIG FOR MAY CONTAIN TRACES OF PEANUTS CD)
UPSTAIRS CHARLIES BAR, 1997.

At the time of this gig Bambi were quite popular on the Dublin punk scene, they had a good following and it was a little bit trendy to say you liked them. They had a good sound of Stooges style punk mixed with organ sounding keyboards and Beastie Boys attitude. Supporting them on this particular night were stalwarts of the DIY scene Jackbeast. They were such an amazing band, they regularly played gigs for the Hope Collective - often benefits for various causes. I had seen them many times and they were always class. Their sound was kind of influenced by Steve Albini sounding bands like Rapeman, Slint and Shellac. They had a no frills attitude they just used to get up on stage play an amazing set, step off into the audience and watch the next band. This particular gig sticks in my memory as it wasn't long before they released their second release, their self titled 10" and they were particularly tight. I remember I had gone to the gig with my girlfriend of the time Jenny and was rude to an ex-girlfriend who was at the gig, which I've always regretted. I suppose one has to live with such regrets...

THE EX/SEA DOG
CRAWDADDY/THE LOWER DECK 2007

This was actually two gigs on the one night. The Ex played in Crawdaddy on Harcourt Street to a full house. It's a posh enough venue for a gig, the sound is usually very good, it's not particularly big so you nearly always get a good position to see the band. The Ex were particularly amazing on this night. They were really tight, the sound was perfect and they played a deadly set. I've seen them once since then but not since they have the new singer as I really liked the old guy GW Sok. I would love to see them again if I get the chance.

As the Ex gig was finishing there was a gig on over the road in The Lower Deck with a couple of bands but my favourite Irish band of the time Sea Dog were timed so as you could leave the Ex and get over for their set. It was perfect. I'm not totally sure if Sea Dog are finished now but they were amazing during their productive peak. They had a 70's influenced stoner rock sound with some lovely 'Lizzy like guitar noodles and face melting back and forth guitar playing (I know Niall is gonna hate that -sorry!). After the first gig, it was class to come across the road to this one and enjoy it with many friends who had been at both gigs or just the later one.

FUGAZI
RED BOX 2002

Fugazi played I think 3 Irish gigs over a week in October 2002. This one in the Red Box in Dublin was by no means the most intimate or DIY, such honours would go to either the Limerick gig or Derry one as part of the same tour. For me this one was my favourite as they played more of my favourite songs by them. I also remember I had a nice bit of space to rock out in and spent the whole gig doing that. Class!

THE DAGDA
CLUB GZ, PARNELL MOONEYS, 2001?

The Dagda played crust punk and were from Belfast. At this stage they were a three piece with one vocalist Glynn, they later had more members and two vocalists. I think I prefered this period. This gig sticks in my mind as it was a couple of days after my Granny died. I had just returned to Dublin from Galway where the funeral was, I think I travelled back by bus and dropped into this gig on the way back to my flat in Phibsboro. There wasn't that many

at the gig, I enjoyed seeing the Dagda but I felt sad about my Granny's passing and removed from the people at the gig, I think I only told my friend Clodagh then. I was glad to be there though and it felt somehow therapeutic.

MUDHONEY
ROME OCT 2009

I was in Rome to get married. [As it happens I first met my wife Aine at a Fuktifino gig in Galway, we became friends and a good while later got together]. A few of my friends were over for the occasion. My friend Jamie being a man with his ear to the ground and who doesn't miss much of what is going on in the underground music world, had discovered that grunge legends Mudhoney were playing two nights before the wedding. We were all there in Rome anyway and what better way to celebrate being there than going to see Mudhoney. I had seen Mudhoney not that long previously when they played in the Village in Dublin, which was the first time they had played in Ireland for about 15 years or so. I believe original bassist Matt Lukin left the band and they had more energy for touring and writing new material. They were full of energy tonight and were really rocking! We had a great spirit of camaraderie and celebration about us, all being in Rome for the one occasion and happening across Mudhoney. A good night for sure!

BIKINI KILL, TEAM DRESCH, BIS
CHARLIES BAR, AUNGIER ST 1996

This was the first DIY punk gig I was ever at, it blew my mind. At that stage in my life I was regularly going to concerts and live music but it was usually to expensive gigs maybe £25 for concerts in The Point Depot or the RDS or £16 for the Olympia or the Mean Fiddler. I hadn't discovered the underground DIY punk scene yet. I had been picking up freesheets (four page free zines/ newsletters) in record shops for a few months and had been interested to discover the gigs. I knew Bikini Kill, firstly because Courtney Love had had a big row with Kathleen Hanna on the Lollapolooza tour some years previously. I also had a tape of their lp *Pussy Whipped*. Bis from Scotland had a hit single *Kandy Pop* which made it onto Top of the Pops, so there was a bit of a buzz about them.

I first saw the gig listed in one of the freesheets but it was also listed on a live music billboard all over town by one of the big drinks companies - Carlsberg or Heineken. It was unknown to me that a gig would only be £3 in. Long story short there was a massive queue outside Charlies bar. I was in the queue with some friends when one of the organisers came down and handed us a printed handout all about the gig collective, the Hope Collective, who had organised the gig and about the various bands they had put on in the past and bootleg tapes they had for sale for £2 each!

Inside the upstairs venue, the place was jammers. There was a merch table set up to one side. The first band Bis played and seemed to get most of the crowd, it was still packed for Bikini Kill and slackened off a bit for Team Dresch (I didn't know them before, but really liked them).

I didn't know Niall McGuirk then (of *React*, Hope and this zine) but I remember seeing a tall guy wearing a Freebird Records t-shirt helping to lift some gear into the band through the packed crowd. That turned out to be him. I had the pleasure to meet him some months later after I had started my zine *Loserdom* and enquired about helping with the Hope Collective. As I say that gig blew my mind!

So many gigs so many favourites,. I could write about many more, actually I've done just that in my next zine *Loserdom #24* which I hope to have out real soon, mark my words!

105.

JAMES HENDICOOT
(FREELANCE JOURNALIST)
A CONVERSATION WITH DROPKICK MURPHYS
2013

The Irish talk more of the export of our culture than the multiculturalism that now graces our streets, but sometimes it takes an outsider to show you what you have is great. Oddly, for me, that man was Dropkick Murphys' Ken Casey.

Working as a journalist, I was granted what turned out to be an extended audience with the longest-serving member of the biggest 'Irish' band not to come from our shores.

The Murphys are widely derided in the Irish music scene. 'Plastic Paddys' or words to the effect of 'folk sacrilege' are merrily chucked in their direction, but Casey's arrival for a press day during which he dedicated over an hour to telling tales of Boston, Ireland and the Boston Irish topped up my sense of wonder.

Casey talked of Tommy Makem, and his insistence that 'The Pogues ruined Irish music,' chuckling at his conservatism. He talked about Ronnie Drew popping up at Murphys show before his death in reverential tones, and almost cries at the story of Drew's backing:

"Don't let anybody tell you you're doing something wrong," Casey reports Drew saying. *"You're doing what you need to do to get the next generation listening. If this is what it's going to take to get the music thriving..."*

There's a 5000 word essay in the stories Casey squeezed into an hour. It takes on Spicy McHaggis' surprisingly adept French language skills, not being able to clap the Boston Red Sox big moments because they play 'Shipping Up To Boston' over the top and it's too embarrassing, and the dangers involved in playing 'Skinhead on the MTA' live. It touches on pride at the Irish rugby team using a Murphys single to introduce games, and regret that he's never been able to relocate.

What struck me, though, was how closely the Murphys' experience matches my own glances at the rough edges that make our music scene great.

"Our banjo player, Jeff, he writes on a blackout at 3am," Casey told me. *"All his song emails come at 3 or 4am and he doesn't remember sending them. But I'll pick them up in the morning, add a vocal melody and we'll have the elements of an idea to work with in the practise room."* That just sounds right.

'Skinhead on the MTA' is an adaption of an Irish American folk song. Like many Murphys songs, it's a folk song for the next generation; a continuation of our culture that happens to have been produced somewhere else.

For some, the Murphys will never be the real thing. They can raise $2 million for charity by having professional baseball players smack them in the face with tomatoes at 90 miles an hour (amongst other things) and cram the stage with the crowd every gig, and they'll never be quite Irish enough. But that's too simple: the music that we love belongs to all of now, especially those who love it too.

There's very little Irish music today that doesn't contain outside influences. If any. The Frames are influenced heavily by Bob Dylan. Paranoid Visions point to Crass, and Two Door Cinema Club to Idlewild and Mew. It should be welcomed with open arms, because it's made our music scene what it is. Murphys, if you like, are the reversal of that, and they stare in with awe.

Like an (aging) newborn foal sat in a hotel lobby fawning over the ordinary, the appreciation implicit in Casey's brief revitalised by enthusiasm for the Dublin scene at a time when I felt it was plodding. What we have isn't clean, or simple, but it is extremely diverse and filled with unbelievable talent, and sometimes we forget that. It's there. Just ask any new arrival.